TEAM
BUILDING

A Structured Learning Approach

TEAM BUILDING

A Structured Learning Approach

PETER MEARS

Department of Management
University of Louisville
Louisville, Kentucky

FRANK VOEHL

Stategy Associates, Inc.
Coral Springs, Florida

S^tL

St. Lucie Press
Boca Raton Boston London New York Washington, D.C.

Preface

This book takes a hands-on approach to developing empowered teams, which are found in all high-performing organizations. It will not be difficult for you to read about the team-building concepts, and the exercises should prove to be enjoyable.

Not everything will be easy, however. It will be difficult for you to practice team-building concepts because most of your previous training probably consisted of reading or memorizing and then simply executing what you learned. That is, learning was not personalized; in fact, your previous instructors may have done everything possible to remove personalities from your learning experiences. For the most part, your previous learning experiences were probably abstract events that never required you to change your behavior.

If you want to learn how to function effectively as a member of a team, then plan on **changing your behavior and your way of thinking**. As a team member, do not think of "your contribution" or the "good points" you added to the discussions. Start thinking in terms of what you did **not** do to move the team forward. It will take practice to acquire this skill, because we often feel that by contributing to the discussion we are contributing to the team. Perhaps you did make a contribution, but the contribution was minor unless it helped the team achieve its goal.

The key to learning how to function effectively as a team member involves much more than simply participating in the discussion. You must learn how to objectively evaluate your impact on the team if you are going to function effectively.

We will take a hands-on approach to learning about quality. After learning quality principles, you will then be asked to apply these principles in a structured environment that is designed to gradually improve your team-building skills. Because team roles constantly change, a structured learning approach will be used to evaluate the interactions of team members so that they can learn how to improve themselves. That is, we are creating an environment in which team members continuously learn how to learn by applying these skills to their jobs.

A multiple learning opportunity is provided here. First, you will learn quality principles. Second, a team environment will be used to apply the skills learned. Third, you will learn how to analyze the effectiveness of a team, so that you can further improve your team skills. Then, when the sessions are completed, you will have taken the first step in the journey toward quality improvement. The next step, applying this knowledge, is up to you.

Acknowledgment

Thanks are due to Dr. Bruce Kemelgor (Associate Professor of Management, University of Louisville) for sharing his years of experience in building organizational teams and for reviewing early copies of the manuscript for this book.

Contents

Chapter 1

Teamwork and Synergy

Why have teams? The answer is simple: you can't do it yourself. Perhaps in early industrial society, with its emphasis on physical labor, most jobs could be done without the interaction of others—but not today. The mix of skills needed to solve most organizational problems is so great that a team effort has become virtually a necessity.

This does not mean that you personally will not benefit from working on teams. Teams can help you in several ways:

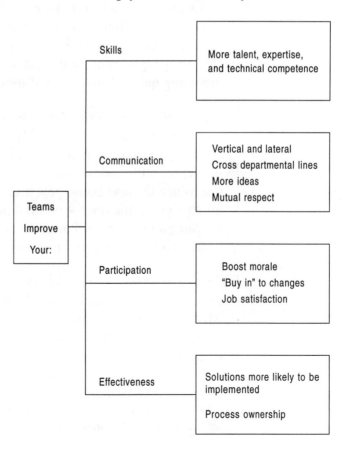

Teams Improve Your:		
	Skills	More talent, expertise, and technical competence
	Communication	Vertical and lateral Cross departmental lines More ideas Mutual respect
	Participation	Boost morale "Buy in" to changes Job satisfaction
	Effectiveness	Solutions more likely to be implemented Process ownership

Once you have mastered teamwork skills, you will be able to improve your overall effectiveness on the job. However, the objective is not simply to learn a few group techniques, because learning will then stop as soon as you put the book down. The objective is to practice the techniques until they become second nature to you. When a group of people working together all have teamwork skills, the group has created a condition where it has learned how to learn. And then you are off and running.

You will "get" more than you "give" to teams. Teams can improve your general skills, enhance your communication ability, give you an opportunity to participate, and most importantly, improve your effectiveness.

The Silly Goose?

When you see geese heading south for the winter, flying in a "V" formation, think about what science has learned about why they fly that way. As each bird flaps its wings, it creates uplift for the bird immediately following it. By flying in a "V" formation, the whole flock can fly at least 71% farther than if each bird flew on its own. Perhaps people who share a common direction can get where they are going quicker and easier if they cooperate.

Whenever a goose falls out of formation, it feels the resistance of trying to go it alone and quickly gets back into formation to take advantage of flying with the flock. If we have as much sense as a goose, we will work with others who are going the same way as we are. When the lead goose gets tired, he rotates back in the wing and another goose flies on the point. It pays to take turns doing hard jobs for our group. Perhaps the geese honking from behind are even the "cheering squad" to encourage those up front to keep up their speed.

Finally, if a goose weakens or is wounded and falls out of formation, two geese fall out and follow him down to help and protect him. They stay with him until he is either able to fly or until he is dead. Then they set out on their own, or with another formation, until they catch up with their group. If we had the sense of a goose, we would stand by each other like that.

Reported in the Association for Quality & Participation, Louisville Kentucky Chapter, September 1992. Original source unknown.

Synergy

"Effectiveness is measured by results!" Ever since Dr. Norman Maier, the father of synergy and group dynamics, issued this principle of getting things done over 20 years ago, the bottom line has remained the same no matter how hard we work or try. We need results, results, results! In today's complex and fast-paced world, achieving results while at the same time maintaining excellence demands the development of high-performance organizational teams.[1] This holds true for schools and universities as much as it does for business, industry, and government organizations.

There are several reasons why high-performing teamwork is crucial to producing effectiveness and excellence:

- Research has shown that groups often make better decisions when issues are difficult.

- When tasks are complex, specialized, and changing, it is impossible for a leader or any one person to know all the relevant information.

- The likelihood of successful implementation can be improved through a well-coordinated team of people working together to help solve one another's problems.

- Quality will be higher when team members can confront each other about problems that are being hidden or information that is being withheld.

- Shared-responsibility teamwork sets the stage for further individual development, which occurs when the team is collectively performing many of the managerial functions involved in running meetings and projects, building the team effort, and managing problem-solving tasks.

- Teams help people learn through direct feedback, which is a valuable source of information and a powerful impetus for change.

Results are a combination of the brainpower of all team members, coupled with the process skills used. When people are able to use their process skills cooperatively, the results go far beyond the sum of their individual efforts. In turn, high accomplishments can create breakthroughs in thinking and become positive models that influence others in the organization. Team membership is a powerful motivational device that can lead to improved quality, productivity, and effectiveness.

In many organizations, roadblocks can occur when specialists protect their areas of interest by hiding behind obsolete methods of operation and following procedures that require numerous approvals by upper management and endless meetings to get even the simplest task accomplished. The organization suffers when tasks cannot be effectively accomplished. Teams, particularly cross-functional teams, can help reduce many of these roadblocks by sharing objectives and a desire to accomplish a task.

What Is Synergy?

Synergy is defined as:

> the interaction of two or more agents or forces so that their combined effort is far greater than the sum of their individual efforts.

In the organizational sense, synergy can be described as a cooperative interaction among groups, especially among parts of a corporation or organization, that creates an enhanced combined effect (from the Greek word *sunergia,* meaning cooperation or working together).

Major Elements of Team Synergy

Several interpersonal skills are required by team members in order for teams to be effective. These skills are based on the team-building simulations developed by the Human Synergistics organization.

Listening and clarifying requires that all team members pay attention and be responsive to the direction taken by the person talking. Do not interpret the speaker, and avoid judging what was said. Concentrate on summarizing and understanding what was said.

Active listening is conspicuous by its absence. Team members may carry on more than one conversation at a time, as well as interrupt one another and jump from one conversation to the next. As a result, vital information gets lost and ideas are not properly explored, which leads to hasty and poor selection of alternatives. The difficulty in listening effectively stems from the fact that the mind thinks three or four times faster than the average person speaks. This creates surplus time with which the brain must deal, which allows extraneous thoughts to creep into the picture. Daydreaming often occurs, as well as "temporary blackouts" of thought pattern. Listening does not come easily to most people. Listening comprehension training has been known to dramatically improve retention rates by using the following four principles:

■ Anticipate where the conversation is going

■ Objectively weigh the information being presented

■ Periodically review and mentally summarize what is being said

■ Pay attention to the non-verbal behavior as well

Speakers are advised to remember the difficulty of listing and can help get their message across to team members by using visual aids. Flip-charts and blackboards can be used to display ideas and improve understanding of what is being said. This will be necessary to obtain "buy in" to the concepts presented.

Supporting involves encouraging people to speak up and creating a positive climate where others will feel free to offer ideas. In a defensive climate, individuals become preoccupied with their own security rather than the growth of the team as a whole. A positive climate is created by truly believing in the fact that everyone is important and can make a contribution to the team. Everyone is therefore treated with respect and all ideas offered are considered, without trying to control or manipulate outcomes.

This may sound simple, but it is difficult to create a supportive environment. Many people tend to shoot first and ask questions later, especially when presented with a new idea. We tend to focus on the negative first, on what is wrong, rather than considering what may be right about the idea. This results in good ideas going unrecognized and people becoming frustrated due to lack of support, thereby reducing team effectiveness.

Differing and confronting skills involve the ability to present conflicting ideas to the group, without threatening any individuals. This involves focusing comments on factual issues and avoiding personalities. There is a place on a team for the "devil's advocate" because if the team cannot answer challenging ideas or comments, perhaps discussion of the item under consideration should not proceed.

Quality as a personal commitment to excellence is essential. Team members must accept their responsibilities, be willing to do quality work, and be willing to pay attention to details. The team cannot succeed unless all members have a personal commitment to excellence.

Acceptance of the idea that each team member brings a potentially valuable mix of skills to the team is needed. Unless each team member is valued as an individual, there will be a reluctance to accept one another's ideas and contributions.

Feedback in terms of open and honest communication is critical to achieving results. We will utilize two types of feedback in this book. Teams will be provided traditional feedback in the form of results, so that they can gauge their effectiveness. In addition, a task observation form will be used whereby a team member assumes the role of an observer and records the interactions of the team. This observer (the role rotates among team members) reports the interactions at the end of a team meeting so that the group members can discuss the dynamics that have occurred in order to improve themselves. An environment is thereby created in which teams learn how to learn.

Do You Need a Team?

To team, or not to team; that is the question! Not all situations are appropriate for teamwork. For example, in a situation where employees are doing solitary work, where there is no requirement for people to coordinate their activities, a team is not needed. Teamwork is really only appropriate in situations that require a high interdependence among individuals, which covers most tasks performed in an organization.

Research[2] has shown that the nature of a team varies with its degree of formality and it permanence. Also, strategies need to be developed for sustaining team behavior, because the introduction of teams into an autocratic environment, where the boss has traditionally made the "important" decisions, will be disastrous. If team members repeatedly try to accomplish something only to find out that the boss disapproves, they will soon give up.

Having made these observations, let's assume that you have decided to move ahead with a teamwork structure. There are four types of teams that you need to be aware of: work teams (formal and permanent), cross-functional project teams (formal and temporary), network teams (informal and permanent), and alliance teams (informal and temporary). (See Chapter 10 for more information on the different types of teams.)

Team Size

Having determined the appropriate type of team for your situation, the key question now becomes how many people should be on the team. In practice, effective teams are actually quite small, with the ideal team size between six to seven people on the average. In controlled experiments with teams of five and twelve individuals, Prof. A. Paul Hare found "that the performance of the groups of five was generally superior."[3] The reason for this stems from the number of transactions, which increases exponentially as the size of the team increases.

When there are more than seven people on a team, the total number of possible interactions among team members is almost unmanageable. On the other hand, when the team is composed of fewer than four or five members, creativity and ideation are minimized. In his seminal work on the American work group, published in 1950, George Humans[4] first advanced the claim that the smaller groups are the most durable, and his argument still holds up 40 years later.

Characteristics of an Effective Team

Questionnaires, surveys, interviews, etc. are used to determine if the members of a group are prepared to make the commitment to become a team. Among other things, a team requires a high level of trust, an open climate for communication, and shared decision making. Major characteristics of an effective team are shown in Table 1. Note that the team is self-conscious about how it functions and will examine how it is performing. Being a member of a high-performance team is not always easy, but it is always challenging.

Should Team Membership Be Voluntary?

Voluntary team membership seems to work best when its purpose is clearly seen as tied to some type of an employee-centered outcome. According to recent research reported in *National Productivity Review,* when the purpose of a voluntary team is tied to achieving only organizational goals, then the effectiveness and longevity of the team diminish.[5] The researcher concluded that people prefer that their participation be required when dealing with organizational issues. From the worker's point of view, requiring participation symbolizes the company's commitment to quality improvement and organizational change.

Achieving Positive Team Synergy

In the synergy model of effectiveness, as in real life, elements that interact with one another affect one another. If any of the elements are less than perfect, then the overall effectiveness of the team is diminished. For example, suppose team effectiveness (E) is the product of the interaction between quality (Q), acceptance (A), and feedback (F) in the formula:

$$E = Q * A * F$$

Table 1

Characteristics of an Effective Team

■ The atmosphere is informal and relaxed, without obvious tensions. People are involved and do not show signs of boredom.

■ There is much discussion in which everyone participates. Discussion is focused. If the discussion gets off track, someone will bring it back.

■ The team's task is understood and accepted by the members. Task objectives are discussed until they are formulated so that team members can become committed.

■ Members listen to each other! The discussion does not jump from one idea to another unrelated idea. Every idea is given a hearing.

■ The team is comfortable with disagreement and does not avoid conflict simply to keep everyone in agreement. Disagreements are not suppressed or overridden by premature action, nor is there a tyranny of the minority. Disagreements are discussed so that solutions can be found.

■ Decisions are reached by a consensus in which it is clear that everyone is in general agreement and willing to go along.

■ Criticism is frequent, frank, and relatively comfortable. There are no personal attacks, either openly or hidden. Criticism is constructive and is oriented toward removing obstacles facing the group.

■ People are free to express their feelings and ideas on the team's problems.

■ When action is taken, clear assignments are made and accepted.

■ The leader does not dominate, nor does the team defer unduly to the leader. Because of their knowledge or experience, different members act as resource leaders without power struggles. The issue is not who controls the team, but instead how to get the job done.

■ The team is self-conscious about how it functions and will examine how it is performing.

To achieve a perfect score of 1.0, we would need to achieve a score of 1.0 for each of the three variables, as follows:

$$E = Q * A * F$$

$$1.0 = 1.0 * 1.0 * 1.0$$

Let's look at what happens when a little less than perfection is achieved. If we are 90% effective in our quality goals, 90% effective in gaining acceptance of the ideas, and 90% effective in feedback, our overall effectiveness would fall to 72%:

$$E = Q * A * F$$

$$0.72 = 0.9 * 0.9 * 0.9$$

Furthermore, if we achieved and are satisfied with a weak performance of 50% in our quality, acceptance, and feedback goals, our overall effectiveness would fall to a miserable 12%:

$$E = Q * A * F$$

$$0.12 = 0.5 * 0.5 * 0.5$$

To make matters even worse, a score of zero in any portion of the formula results in total effectiveness being zero:

$$E = Q * A * F$$

$$0.0 = 1.0 * 0.0 * 1.0$$

For example, we could have a high-quality computerized information system, with excellent feedback to users, but if the users do not accept the system, its effectiveness is zero. This is despite the fact that we had a perfect score in quality and the specs and documentation requirements (feedback) were also excellent. Acceptance is critical in all types of systems,[6] including quality systems.

To complete the analogy, let's also look at why relationships fail:

$$E = Q * A * F$$

$$0.0 = 1.0 * 1.0 * 0.0$$

When feedback in the form of meaningful communication fails, then the relationship falls apart, whether the relationship is a marriage or a business team. Therefore, in order to improve synergy in a positive manner, acceptance and buy-in are critical at an early stage. Coupled with designing feedback channels into the way the team operates, this will go a long way toward ensuring effectiveness.

What Have I Gotten Into?

Provided you are willing to learn how to work with others as a team member, and if you are also willing to modify your behavior in order to improve the effectiveness of the team, you are in for an exciting experience. Groups may vary, but all tend to go through multiple stages,[7] often known as:

Forming: The initial orientation

Storming: A stage of conflict and confusion

Norming: A stage of consolidation around tasks

Performing: A stage of teamwork and performance

Forming is the initial stage when the team is first formed. When team members first come together, they are cautious, and there is bound to be some anxiety about what lies ahead.

Storming occurs when team members realize that the task to be performed is difficult and participants tend to rely on their own experience, as they have done in the past. There is resistance to working openly with some team members, and there is a tendency to form cliques. Many members will be impatient about the team's progress on the task assigned.

Norming occurs when team members start to help one another. A sense of team cohesion develops as members begin to understand each other's strengths and weaknesses. In this stage, members are friendly to one another and work together to overcome conflict.

Performing occurs when the team has matured. Team members understand their strengths and weaknesses and are satisfied with the team's progress. Members know how to deal with complex tasks and can handle interpersonal conflicts.

Endnotes

1. The concept of high-performance teams creating excellence and effectiveness was introduced by Bradford and Cohen in their book entitled *Managing for Excellence* (New York: John Wiley and Sons, 1984). Their portrait of a mature, shared-responsibility team was as early wake-up call for managers eager to learn the differences between teams and groups.

2. The Centre for the Study of Management Learning at the University of Lancaster, England has done extensive research in team appropriateness and has published its findings in Vol. 23, Part 4, pp. 349–362, 1992. These findings are documented in an article by Malcom Higgs and Deborah Rowland called "All Pigs Are Equal?" cited in the above-mentioned publication.

3. Paul Hare, "A Study of Interaction and Consensus in Different Sized Groups," *American Sociological Review,* Vol. 17, pp. 261–268, June 1952.

4. George Humans, *The Human Group* (New York: Harcourt, Brace), 1950.

5. In the spring of 1992, *National Productivity Review* published an article by Richard Magjuka entitled "Should Membership in Employee Involvement (E.I.) Programs Be Voluntary?" The author reviewed several research studies based upon thousands on surveys and interviews on the effects on performance of membership in these programs, also called Quality Action Teams (QATs) in the studies. The studies pointed out that what started as voluntary often became a way to reach organizational goals.

6. The concept of the synergistic effect of quality and acceptance was first introduced by Dr. Norman Maier in one of his early works, *Principles of Human Behavior* (New York: John Wiley, 1952). This concept was expanded in the work by J.J. Hayes entitled *Creative Management* (New York: John Wiley, 1962). He followed up this concept in *Problem Solving Discussions and Conferences* (New York: McGraw-Hill, 1963).

7 . The early idea of Forming, Storming, Norming, and Performing was developed by Bruce Tuckman in 1955 in his article entitled "Development Sequence in Small Groups," which appeared in *Psychological Bulletin.*

Exercise 1

Knowing Your Team Members

Behavioral objectives:

To get to know the members of the team better and to develop an appreciation of the diversity and wealth of knowledge among the different members.

Time limit:

35 minutes

Instructions:

Let's direct our attention to finding out some personal details about our fellow team members. A team can be particularly powerful if it includes members with diverse skills and if all members respect each other's skills.

Interview one person on your team and, in turn, be interviewed by that person. Find out about the person's background and any unique hobbies, skills, or unusual interests he or she may have. You have ten minutes to conduct the interview and be interviewed by that person. Record this information in the space provided. Use this time to "get comfortable" with the person you are interviewing.

Then get back together in your team. Introduce the person you interviewed to the team (and in turn be introduced to the team) and explain this person's background, including at least one unique interest identified in the interview.

Exercise 1

Team Interview
Team Member's Name:
Background:
Hobbies/Interests:
Unique Interests:

Detach at perforation

Chapter 2

Contributors to Continuous Quality Improvement

Various names and acronyms have been used to identify the concept of Continuous Quality Improvement (CQI). Some organizations call their quality improvement efforts Total Quality Management (TQM). Other organizations call their improvement efforts Quality Improvement (QI) or simply Total Quality (TQ).

The acronym CQI will be used throughout this book, to avoid the perception that quality improvement is simply another management program. CQI is not a program; it is a long-term philosophy where everyone works together to improve the quality of an organization's goods and services. A team effort is required for meaningful quality improvement to occur, and, as we shall soon see, a team is far more than a group of people getting together.

History of Industrial Teams

Early studies of industrial work groups, such as the Hawthorne studies of Dr. Elton Mayo,[1] suggested that the group provided the workers with only marginal motivation to be more productive. Indeed, evidence suggests that working in the old ways has little impact on individual productivity. If the group is to be a truly effective force in motivating the individual worker, group members must be given "responsible autonomy" to make decisions about important aspects of the group's work assignments. On the other hand, sometimes management becomes very concerned about and resistant to relaxing traditional controls over the primary work groups.

This is due to a fear of production slowdown, coupled with the risk of increased overall cost to the organization despite the productivity of individual team efforts. Team coordination became a major problem for management teams during the latter part of the 1960s and the 1970s, before the age of the TQM contributors.[2] Pre-TQM research workers such as Maier, Likert, and McGregor realized that their techniques had to be linked to the organizational framework. Likert used what he called "overlapping group families" and "linking pin" functions to tie the participation of teams to all levels within the organization. Similarly, Maier's new direction for organizations envisioned participation in problem-solving conferences at all levels through overlapping membership on all types of teams (vertical, diagonal, and horizontal). This was a precursor to the TQM notion of cross-functional teamwork.

Starting in the 1960s, the concept of T-group (T stands for training) was introduced in the U.S. by Edgar Schein and Kurt Lewin, while in Japan the Quality Circle movement was initiated by Professor Kauro Ishikawa. Schein introduced the general "Theory of Influence," which held that superficial skills and knowledge are relatively easy to change in bits and pieces, whereas attitudes must be changed in large chunks or not at all. Because attitudes tend to hang together in large interlocking systems, changing only one attitude tends to create cognitive dissonance. A team member may therefore try to restore consistency to his or her attitudes more easily by rejecting the new paradigm than by rejecting or replacing all the old ones.

Kurt Lewin initiated an era of rigorous laboratory studies into the dynamics of how groups function. The most impressive aspects of his studies focused on the Harwood Manufacturing Company, with its teams of machinists involved in democratic methods and group decision making.

While the Harwood results were not effectively duplicated through other research experiments, the die was cast. In 1947, Lewin helped found the Bethel National Training Lab, which eventually led to the T-group movement of the 1950s and 1960s. During the 1950s, new training programs were developed by those looking for new roles for the behavioral sciences as the emphasis continued to shift from individual change to group development. Such established and emerging experts as Maslow, Argyis, Bennis, Bradford, Gibb, and Benne were joined in ranks by the Employee Relations Department of Esso, under the leadership of Robert Blake and Jan Mouton, as well as H.A. Sheppard from the Southwest Human Relations Lab of the University of Texas.[3]

Meanwhile, behavioral researchers Bion, Jaques, Trist, Rice and others in the United Kingdom performed studies under the guidance of the Tavistock Institute of Human Relations in London, centering around the Glacier Metal research project which began in 1948 and ran in some fashion for ten years. Their research focused on the emotional life of the team and various levels of cooperation which, Bion taught, always functioned at two levels: the conscious level towards its work task and the unconscious level towards satisfaction of powerful emotional drives. Bion believed that the team acted as if it had certain basic assumptions about its aims, which he termed dependence, fight-flight, and pairing. These were the source of emotional drives far different from their task objectives. They are derived from a very primitive level and need to be addressed and successfully discussed and defined in order for the group to be productive and effective. This eventually led to the concept of Autonomous Work Groups, which provided a mechanism to deal with the problems of worker motivation, participation, and power equalization and provided a new role for the team/work group far different from that advocated by Mayo, Lewin, and Likert.[4]

The success of the Tavistock experiments highlighted the failure of research workers and management in general to make basic changes in organizational structure and in the nature and organization of the work, in order to provide greater autonomy and worker self-control. Teams provided an answer to this problem by offering a method of improving autonomy and control over work activities and, if the project is challenging, enhanced task/job content coupled with basic management skills as well. This eventually led to the work of the TQM contributors during the 1960s and beyond, and the teams process was a key component of their teachings and success.

We will learn what the three main quality contributors have to say, and then continue the process of team building by applying these principles to practical organizational problems. Principles underlying quality improvement have evolved through the efforts of several major contributors, including Deming, Crosby, and Juran. A summary of the principles offered by each will be presented in the sections that follow.

Continuous Quality Improvement (CQI)

- Overview

  - Deming

    - Crosby

      - Juran

        - Malcolm Baldrige National Quality Award

Concepts flow from Deming

CQI is...

Continuous improvement in satisfying customers

Reducing the variation in products or services

Notice how the concepts flow from Dr. Deming. These contributors view quality slightly differently, but they approach the subject from an application viewpoint. That is, they do not view quality in abstract, theoretical terms, but rather in terms that make the concept operational. Therefore, a two-part operational definition of CQI will be used throughout this book:

Continuous Quality Improvement is:

■ Continuous improvement in satisfying customers

■ Reducing variation in the products or services produced

In the summaries which follow, the word *product* is used to mean both products and services. Products can be either tangible (i.e., a product such as a new car or a service such as income tax advice) or intangible (the satisfaction or pleasure derived from purchasing and using the product).

When reading these summaries, think about how each contributor would evaluate:

1. An organization's use of its human resources

2. The role of management

3. The concept of reduction of variation in the processes that produce goods and services

4. The methods used by an organization to continuously improve the quality of its goods and services

Deming's Guide to Quality Improvement

Dr. W. Edwards Deming believes there are three major *keys* to quality improvement. The first key is that everyone should understand and use statistics to identify variations that occur in the process and the products (including services) produced. Deming views statistics as a common language that all employees, from top management to the hourly worker, can use to communicate with one another. Statistics is objective and provides a clear basis for communicating between different managerial levels in order to reduce misunderstanding. The use of statistics will help employees identify the cause of product variations, so that these variations can be studied and eliminated.[5]

In other words, Deming believes that variation itself is wrong. The causes of product and process variation must be identified and eliminated so that the right product is produced the right way, every time.

Deming's second key to quality improvement is that management must accept the fact that it is responsible for quality because it owns the process. Deming pulls no punches here. He believes that management, particularly management in the United States, has failed to live up to its responsibility by fully accepting the fact that it is responsible for poor product quality. Management's job is to lead an organization in a never-ending, continuous improvement of quality. Never-ending improvement is achieved by a continual reduction of variation in the processes that produce a product or service. It is not a "quick-fix" solution of appointing blame when something goes wrong.

Deming believes that we know we are working in organizations that are not producing high-quality goods and services. This results in stress because we know we could be doing better. Stress leads to problems on the job as well as personal problems (drug and alcohol abuse, family strife). Consequently, the effect of poor management is creeping into our lives and is pervasive in our culture.

Deming's third key is that all work is performed as part of a system, which can be organized in any number of ways to best satisfy customer requirements. One of these ways, which the Japanese perfected, is through work teams. Dr. Deming believes that everyone can perform an active, meaningful role on a team to improve the work system by improving the input and output of all stages of the system.

Dr. Deming suggests that, where appropriate, the teams should be comprised of members from different staff and line areas. He emphasizes that the team has a customer, just like anyone else, and the team should identify whether or not it is meeting the requirements of its customers. He goes on to stress that all team members must have a chance to contribute their ideas, and he worries that the best ideas may become submerged by consensus.

Dr. Deming urges team members to never give up, because their ideas may have a chance the next time around in the improvement cycle. Finally, Deming saw a point in the future when teams will be skilled enough to tear up old ideas, reject what they developed in previous sessions, and start fresh with clear, innovative ideas. Dr. Deming[6] offers some twenty questions to help a team get started. These questions are grouped into four general categories relating to the organization, the team member, customer concerns, and supplier concerns. He concludes this section with the following idea: "Things are happening. The clock is moving rapidly and the time is near when the whole world of people will work as teams with one another."

Dr. Deming offers several general quality questions to guide managers in positioning a firm.

General Quality Questions

■ How many managers has your firm had in the last ten years?

■ Does your firm have a long-term orientation? Does it develop and communicate plans for the future and work toward a better life?

■ Does your firm have a mission statement that is known and lived by all employees?

■ Does your mission statement reinforce your firm as something you should identify with?

■ Does your firm deserve admiration?

■ What is your firm doing to drive out fear and to break down barriers between departments?

■ Do employees have pride in their work?

Deming identifies three major types of quality:

Quality of design	Consumer research: Why do customers come to your firm? Did you ever conduct a consumer attitude survey?
Quality of conformance	Extent to which a firm and its suppliers are able to surpass the design specifications required to meet customer needs.
Quality of performance	Evaluate how well the product performs, then redesign the product to perform even better.

Deming's 14 Points

1. Create consistency of purpose

Create consistency of purpose toward improvement of services with a plan to improve your competitive position. Deming uses the term *mission statement* to include both a vision and the mission statement. He believes that quality improvement begins with a meaningful mission statement that employees and investors can buy into. This includes four levels: organizational, departmental, team, and individual.

A mission statement should address:

Investors	Customers
Employees	Citizenship (community)
Quality philosophy	Distribution of profits
Plans for growth	Fields of interest
Direction (long term)	Corporate objectives (long term)

A mission statement is a living document created with two-way communication. Without a clear, well-understood mission statement that everyone buys into, the organization will flounder, without a sense of direction. Unfortunately, most mission statements are not well known and well understood by employees. For example, could you write an interpretation of the mission statement of either your current or former employer?

Sample topics in a mission statement:

People:

Employees are an asset

Training is a continuous process for all

Teamwork is emphasized

Responsibility, authority, and accountability are delegated as closely as possible to those performing the work

Vacancies are filled from within

Job security

Customers:

Their satisfaction will determine our future existence

Long-term relationships

Employees are encouraged to become involved with customers' needs

Suppliers:

Long-term/single-source if appropriate

Community:

Do we conduct business ethically?

Are we a positive influence?

Is the community really aware of what we do?

Vendors:

Are we purchasing the best?

2. Adopt the new philosophy

We can no longer live with accepted levels of defects, delays, or mistakes. Defects are not free. Someone gets paid for making them. Quality is defined as surpassing customer needs and expectations throughout the life of the product or service. Because we create an arm's-length relationship with our vendors, it is easier to lay blame on them. (We should manage for success, not for failure.)

The attitude of management and employees must be that quality is built in. You cannot inspect for defects after the fact. Everyone should be alert as to why workmanship is less than perfect and should work together to correct the problems. Quality and cost effectiveness are not opposing goals.

Check the effectiveness of your organization's quality:

■ How do you define customer quality?

■ Do your employees know what constitutes high customer quality?

■ How do you know you are pursuing high quality?

■ What do your customers think of your quality compared with other firms in the industry?

Management cannot possibly define customer quality without survey information about the customer's needs and expectations.

3. Cease dependence on mass inspection

Require statistical evidence that quality is built in. Deming stresses the need for statistical controls on all processes. Inspection neither improves nor guarantees quality. It does not make goods better, nor does inspection improve the process. Teamwork and partnering are needed between the firm and its suppliers for process improvements that will improve the quality of goods and services produced. Deming asks: "How do your suppliers find out if they are not meeting your needs or requirements? Are you working closely with them to fulfill your obligation with them?"

4. End the practice of awarding business on the basis of the price tag

Develop detailed measures of quality along with price. Firms often concentrate on developing technical specifications and ignore performance specifications (which include customer satisfaction). These are not equivalent. For example, in serving a steak in a restaurant, the important measurement is customer satisfaction, not the technical specifications (serving an eight-ounce steak). We take the easy way out because performance specifications are difficult and because they include many variables in addition to the technical specification (the size of the steak).

Procurement personnel must learn statistical methods in order to assess quality and make decisions. Communicating back to the vendor is a key element in improving quality. Only in a single-source relationship will a vendor be willing to modify his process to meet revised quality of design specifications at a reasonable price. In addition, there are hidden costs when a firm uses multiple vendors. These costs include variations among different vendors and higher cost in general because each vendor is just beginning the learning curve cycle (i.e., high production hours are spent on each smaller production run).

Statistical Quality Control (SQC) should be applied to all processes and all vendor-supplied items to provide a satisfactory level of evidence of quality. Lawyers should also be trained in the Deming philosophy so that contracts encourage the pursuit of quality rather than foster an attitude of "suing for breach of contract." Supplier teams of a cross-organizational nature should be created to solve problems related to improving process yields.[7]

5. Find problems

It is management's job to work on continually improving the system. This point is the key to understanding Deming's philosophy. Deming stresses that **any** process or product variation is bad. There are two types of variation: special causes (special variation), which are under the control of the operator, and common causes (common variation), which are common to the system and beyond the ability of the operator to control.

Statistics can assist in identifying the causes of variation, which must be sought out and eliminated. Business schools must teach statistical methods for quality control in which everyone in the organization participates under the direction of a competent statistician.

Sources of Process (System) Variation:

Special: These variations are due to an assignable or specific cause. (Deming believes that only 6% of all variations are due to special causes.) Train the operator to find these variations and make the necessary adjustments, such as readjusting the machine under the operator's control. After all special variations are eliminated, the process is considered to be stable. However, the process may still have too many rejects due to common variation.

Common: The cause of 94% of all variation. These are system problems and management owns the system. **Employees just work within the system and cannot change it.**

Deming constantly reinforces an important point: **A process is in control only when it can be controlled by the worker.** Management must eliminate all common variation so that the worker can concentrate on eliminating the special variation that is under his or her control.

Common variation (management's problem) is caused by:

■ Hasty designs, quick answers to customers

■ Inadequate testing of incoming materials and waiving specifications

■ Failure to know the capabilities of the process that are in a state of statistical control

■ Failure to provide workers with statistical signals that will tell them how they are doing and when to make changes

■ Other factors such as smoke, noise, unnecessary dirt, poor lighting, humidity, confusion

---

Control charts can help the operator separate common variations (which should be called to the attention of management) from special variations (which the operator should be trained to control). Upper Control Limit (UCL) and Lower Control Limit (LCL) charts are useful in separating common and special variations. If each operator would eliminate the special variations that are under his or her control, then only common variation, due to variations in the process, would remain. Thus, management would know the capabilities of the process and would be able to work to bring the process under control.

Advantages of a stable process:

■ Management knows the process capability and can predict its performance, cost, and quality levels

■ Production is at a maximum and costs at a minimum

■ Management has data to back up its argument to change specifications

---

A stable process (a process having only common variations) that produces too many defects will do so as long as the system remains the same. Since only management can change the system, the process cannot be improved until management bring the process into statistical control. Statistical tools include flowcharts, check sheets, Pareto analysis, brainstorming, fishbone (cause-and-effect) diagrams, histograms, scatter diagrams, and control charts.

Most poor quality is created by common causes inherent in the production system. Poorly designed services, inadequately trained workers, and poor working conditions are under management, not employee, control. Management is at fault and must develop a stable process. Then, after a stable process has been developed, employees can be held accountable for isolated special causes (i.e., employees can only reduce those variations which are under their control).

6. Institute modern methods of training

People want to do a good job, but often do not know how. It is management's responsibility to help them. All employees should be trained in statistical or TQM-related tools for quality problem solving. This training results in improvements in quality and productivity and also improves employee morale.

When developing a training program:

■ Identify the objectives of the firm

■ Identify goals that will be met through training (a possible goal could be for everyone to understand and meet the mission statement)

■ Orient new employees

■ Train supervisors in statistical thinking

■ Develop/instigate team building

■ Analyze what needs to be taught

■ Only after carefully analyzing what needs to be taught, develop training programs

---

7. Institute modern methods of supervision

Employees are frequently penalized for problems in the system, in which case they are being blamed for things beyond their control. Management must provide customer feedback to employees and must develop an open, supportive atmosphere where there is mutual trust and where employees do not fear management.

Questions for consideration:

■ Does management feel that employees must be policed or else they will slack off and productivity will decrease?

■ Do employees fear management because interactions are generally blaming sessions?

■ Are employees aware of how their jobs fit into the extended process?

■ Are awards/punishments based on common variation (i.e., system variations over which the employee has no control)?

Supervision should be the link between management and the work force. Managers should instigate teamwork by serving as coaches, not policemen.

8. Drive out fear so everyone may work effectively

Most people find work unpleasant, not because they don't like what they do, but because of the climate in which they do it. Fear comes from a feeling of being powerless because a boss has control over important aspects of your life.

9. Break down barriers between departments: everyone in every area must work as a team

The structure of a firm creates barriers between departments and barriers between areas within departments. These barriers must be removed, and cross-functional teams are a useful way to accomplish this task. When there are too many restrictions on communication, too many administrative levels, too much fear of performance appraisals, or numerous quotas, employees often have a negative attitude.

10. Eliminate numerical goals, posters, and slogans that seek new levels of productivity without improving methods

Horrible posters that hold employees accountable for meeting vague goals:

- Do it right the first time
- Safety is job one
- Be careful
- Our job is quality
- Increase sales 10%
- Increase profits

Management must make changes to the production system so that people can meet the goal of improving the quality of the products and services they produce. As long as the process continues to be stable, the same number of defects will be produced. Zero defects is a hollow phrase and a highway to nowhere. Zero variability is the critical component of the system.

11. Eliminate work standards that prescribe numeric quotas

Quotas do not provide a road map for improvement, but instead prohibit good supervision and training. Workers are encouraged to produce goods that may contain defects just to meet quotas. Quotas do not take common and special variation into consideration as a basis for taking action to improve the process.

Get rid of MBO (Management by Objectives)

MBO is just a method to legitimize arbitrary numerical goals. Using MBO, management typically breaks down the "grand plan" into smaller subsections, which are assigned to an individual to achieve. Note that the employees are not given any new tools; they must scavenge from the existing system to meet goals. Increases that are "negotiated" are arbitrary.

12. Remove barriers that rob employees of pride of workmanship

The United States is an underdeveloped nation. We are not using workers to their fullest potential because we rob them of their right to have pride in their work. Because management is not responsive and does not work with employees to improve the process, employees often feel that loyalty to a firm is misplaced and that their energies should be devoted to their families and personal priorities.

If employees do not understand the firm's mission and what is expected of them, they will be confused and unable to identify with the firm. Although the system is at fault, the employee often receives a below average performance appraisal. This results in anger, disloyalty, and loss of pride.

Barriers that rob employees of their pride of workmanship:

■ Managerial ignorance concerning common and special variation

■ Performance appraisal systems destroy teamwork by encouraging people to focus on individual goals rather than organizational goals

■ Daily production reports that focus on yesterday's production without any acknowledgment of variation

■ Failure to identify the cost of quality in terms of visible costs and hidden costs

---

Get Rid of Performance Appraisals

Employees and most managers do not like performance appraisals and view them as a necessary evil. Employees become concerned with obtaining a good performance rating instead of being concerned with what is best for the organization.

Forced performance appraisal systems are the worst! These evaluation procedures state that only 10% of the employees can be evaluated in the top category, only 25% in next category, etc. This process is absurd and must stop being used.

Performance appraisal systems do not distinguish between the performance of the people and the influence of the system on the people. Employees are often held responsible for outcomes of a process they cannot change. An employee reacts to a performance evaluation and changes his or her behavior in order to earn a better rating for the next rating period. If variation was understood, the employee is probably reacting to a common variation which is beyond his or her ability to control. By adjusting behavior, an employee is actually creating more variation in the system.

Employee promotion should be based on the employee's ability to work as a team member. Statistical distributions will highlight that only two out of one thousand people are truly superior or truly inferior. Performance evaluation systems damage the motivation and commitment of the majority of a firm's employees because of the feeling of helplessness brought about by being held accountable for activities over which they have no control.

13. Institute a vigorous program of education and training

Statistical training, communication, future oriented—These terms reinforce Deming's concern with an educated work force. This 13th point refers to continuing, broad education for self-development. Deming's sixth point (previously discussed) refers to training in specific job skills.

14. Create a program that will push the prior 13 points each day for never-ending improvement

Create a cycle of successes with strong management backing for quality. A statistical leader is needed to encourage management to use statistical thinking in decision making.

Exercise 2

Deming's Audit

Behavioral objectives:

To become aware of the group's dynamics. To learn that each member must contribute to the team and must move the conversation forward. The leader must balance the opportunity to contribute and should avoid taking part in the conversation.

Time limit:

45 minutes

Instructions:

After studying Deming's 14 points, get together in your assigned team. Appoint a temporary team leader. The team leader is primarily a coordinator and should avoid taking part in the discussion (or should at least take a minimal role). The primary task of the team leader is to ensure that all members have an opportunity to make a contribution. All team members are to sit close to one another and face each other so that eye contact can easily be made. Everyone is to introduce himself or herself to other members of the team. It is each team member's job to write down the names of fellow team members and to remember these names. Record these names on the form provided for Exercise 2.

Exercise 2

The first job of the leader is to guide the team in selecting one of the following organizations to be audited:

Detach at perforation

> **Typical organizations for auditing:**
>
> Any powerful competitor
>
> A local government agency
>
> University advising system
>
> Local gas station
>
> Local grocery store

For purposes of this exercise, each person is to pretend he or she is Deming. Then take ten minutes and privately write down what you think Deming would say were the three strongest and three weakest points of the organization. Use the form provided. Do **not** simply go over Deming's 14 points. Assume that you are using his quality principles and that you are speaking to the president of the organization. Please be innovative and be prepared to discuss your selections when you meet again with your team.

Exercise 2

Team Members and Deming's Audit Results

Team members:

Deming would identify the following as the three strongest points:

1.

2.

3.

Deming would identify the following as the three weakest points:

1.

2.

3.

Exercise 2

After privately recording what Deming would say are the organization's three strongest and three weakest points, get back together in your team. Try to reach a general team consensus (general agreement) on what Deming would say are the three strongest and three weakest points. Do not resort to voting to reach this agreement.

If there is sufficient time, the team should also try to reach general agreement on what Deming would say regarding:

1. The organization's use of its human resources

2. The role of management

3. How the organization goes about reducing variations in the processes that produce goods and services

4. The methods used by an organization to continuously improve the quality of its goods and services

Crosby's Guide to Quality Improvement

Do you talk about a need for a meaningful, ongoing quality program at your firm? Do you agree that there is a problem, but put off doing anything? If so, then you have identified the problem with quality: it is something everyone talks about, but no one is willing to fully commit to the improvement process.

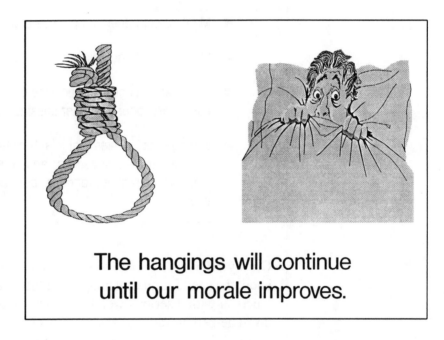

The hangings will continue
until our morale improves.

Profile of a problem firm:

- Employees grumble and complain about poor services and poor food

- Support staff is grumpy about "everything"

- There has been an increase in customer complaints

- Management does not provide a clear definition of quality

- Mentality: schedule first, cost second, quality third

- Management does not know the price of nonconformance: lost customers, poor customer satisfaction, changing staff

- Management denies that it is the cause of the problem. Management makes speeches, and sends everyone to management development programs, but does not make meaningful changes

Crosby offers an example to help us understand this process of talking about the need for quality but putting off meaningful action. What does a person with a serious weight problem or a serious drinking problem do? The person rationalizes the seriousness of the problem and postpones taking action. The only time some people will take action is after they have had a major physical illness or if you can prove to them that they are confronting likely death.

Crosby is the "father" of the Zero Defects (ZD) approach to quality. As an example, if an overweight person wants to gain control of his or her weight, then no fatty foods can be tolerated. Likewise, an alcoholic attempting to change his or her behavior must take a ZD approach to alcohol (i.e., no drinking is permitted).

Organizations are no different. They must develop the attitude that they will not tolerate defects. Anything less than a ZD approach will result in less than an organization's total commitment to improving its quality, and without this total commitment, improvement is unlikely.

Employee "demotivation" is common, prompting management to become concerned about motivation and getting people enthused. What really happened? Didn't we hire motivated people? Why did they become demotivated after working for us? Employees become disillusioned with a firm and its management through the normal, irritating unconcerned ways in which they are treated.

Poor management practices that irritate employees:

■ Performance reviews are a one-way street; dishonest evaluations show people that the firm has no integrity

■ Excessive expense account rules: an eternal battle with the Accounting Department

■ Meetings where the boss rules, i.e., be a faithful listener

■ Bosses who do not really listen to their employees

Hassled People Do Not Produce Quality Work!

Employees who feel hurt or unappreciated sometimes do little work at all. Hassle results in many employees spending more time protecting themselves than they do making something happen.

You do **not** want a program to eliminate hassle. Eating a sandwich is a program; raising children is a process. You are never done with a process.

Many firms do not succeed with quality programs because they are not determined enough. Typical symptoms are shown below.

Symptoms of an Unsuccessful Quality Program:

■ The effort is called a program rather than a process (this encourages people to just go through the motions)

■ Effort is aimed at the lower-level employees in the firm

■ People are cynical when the concept of quality is discussed

■ Management is impatient for results

Crosby defines quality as simply conformance to requirements. Establish the highest possible standards, and then conform to them. Management must ensure that requirements are developed and clearly understood by everyone. Then management must remove procedures and other obstacles that get in an employee's way.

DIRFT (Do It Right the First Time!). This is compatible with the ZD approach of simply not tolerating errors.

The System of Quality Is Prevention. Look at the process and identify opportunities for error. Use Statistical Quality Control (SQC) to identify critical process variables. Measure these variables and adjust the process as required. U.S. management has difficulty allowing employees to accept control. Because managers cannot stand to let employees adjust the process, SQC has not been fully accepted in the United States.

The Performance Standard Must Be Zero Defects

There is **no** acceptable level of defects. A typical payroll department cannot make mistakes because people will not tolerate errors in their paychecks. Imagine the confusion that would occur if an employee were consistently underpaid and had to ask for the money that was rightfully due him or her; the damage to morale would be enormous.

Even if an organization produces 99% of its products/services correctly, that is not good enough! If there are 100 parts in a process, and if each is 99% good (of acceptable quality), the process is capable of making a good product only 34% of the time. (Multiplying 0.99 times itself 100 times yields 0.34.)

Of course, there is a problem getting people to commit to making zero defects. We have all been conditioned throughout our lives to accept the fact that people are not perfect and will therefore make mistakes. We accept errors as a way of life and as a way of doing business. This acceptance of errors is the reason we do not produce high-quality goods and services. Mistakes are caused by lack of knowledge and lack of attention.

The Measurement of Quality Is the Price of Nonconformance

The price of nonconformance includes all expenses involved in doing things wrong. This can be 35% of our costs. Crosby identifies numerous items, including possible loss of customers, to highlight the high hidden cost of poor quality.

Similar to Deming, Crosby has faith in the innate desire of employees to perform their jobs well. Also like Deming, Crosby presents 14 points for improving quality, as shown on the next page. The general role for teams in the Crosby approach is known as Quality Action Teams or QATs at the worker level. At the management level, his teams are called Quality Councils. He sees teams as a way to motivate those who have retarded their own intellectual growth by relying on clichés and habits and have let their minds run on idle. In teams, we can learn from one another.[8] Crosby urges people to leave their footprints in the sand, instead of just dust. He sees teams as a way to change the culture of the organization from a fire-fighting approach to a fire-prevention mode. Crosby was the first of the quality gurus to challenge organizations to unlock their potential. He was also an early proponent, along with Dr. Juran, of the use of the Quality Council as a key to expanding the team's infrastructure to all levels of the organization.

Steps in quality improvement:

1 Appoint a management committee

2 Establish a quality improvement team

3 Set up measurements

4 Identify the cost of poor quality

5 Develop quality awareness

6 Undertake corrective action programs

7 Zero defects planning

8 Employee education

9 Implement a zero defects kickoff day

10 Begin quality goal setting

11 Practice error-cause removal

12 Give recognition to accomplishments

13 Develop a quality council

14 Do it over again

For additional ideas, see Philip B. Crosby, *Quality Without Tears: The Art of Hassle-Free Management* (New York: New American Library), 1984.

Exercise 3

Crosby's Audit

Behavioral objectives:

To think in terms of how your behavior does or does not contribute to the group. All team member must actively contribute equally. There are to be no dominant members, and there are to be no "quiet" group members.

Do not vote on issues. You are trying to reach a consensus (a general agreement) that everyone can live with.

Time limit:

35 minutes

Instructions:

Get together in your assigned team. The role of team leader must be rotated for each exercise, so that everyone on the team has an opportunity to serve as a leader. The new leader should guide the team in selecting and auditing an organization, with each team member pretending that he or she is Crosby. The same organization selected in Exercise 2 may be used, or you may select a new organization. The team leader is to introduce himself or herself to each member of the team. Each team member is to make eye contact with the leader, shake his or her hand, and clearly state his or her own name. From now on, rotate team leadership for each exercise.

After the organization is selected, each member is to take ten minutes to privately write down what Crosby would identify as the organization's three strongest and three weakest points. Use the form provided. Then get back together in your assigned team and reach a general consensus on the three strongest and weakest points.

© St. Lucie Press

Exercise 3

Crosby's Organizational Audit Results

Three strongest points:

1.

2.

3.

Three weakest points:

1.

2.

3.

Detach at perforation

Juran's Guide to Quality Improvement

Dr. Joseph Juran takes the position that no one is against quality. The issue confronting management is how to achieve it. The answer is that management must learn how to manage for quality. The way to manage for quality is to approach quality as if it were as important as a major financial problem confronting an organization.

If an organization had a financial problem, management would install a three-step process:

1. **Financial planning:** Set business financial goals, develop the actions and resources needed to meet the goals, translate the goals into money, and summarize them in the financial plan or budget.

2. **Financial controls:** Evaluate actual performance, compare actual performance to goals, and then take action on the differences. Actions such as cost control or expense control would be used.

3. **Financial improvement:** Do better than in the past. Examples include cost reduction, purchase of facilities to raise productivity, acquisitions, etc.

Middle management has formal goals, budgets, and review processes (including merit ratings) for financial and accounting numerical items. This structured legitimate systems approach must be applied to quality on an ongoing basis.

Management often does not realize how long implementation will take. Managers tend to "start up" a program (not an ongoing process) and then delegate their portion of the process. Quality is not simply a monthly team meeting. It is an activity that is fully integrated into everyone's job.

Managing for Quality: Trilogy Overview

1. Quality Planning

Set business quality goals and develop the means for meeting those goals. Poor planning is the source of poor quality. Planning improvements can occur only with feedback, such as design review, mortality tables (i.e., lessons learned), etc.

Quality is defined as meeting customer expectations. This is accomplished by:

■ Identifying your specific customers

■ Determining customer needs

■ Developing product features to meet customer needs

■ Establishing product goals

■ Developing processes to meet the product goals

■ Providing feedback

2. Quality Control

Run the process in order to meet the product or service goals. In most firms, people do not have the means for improvement. The best they can do is to meet what is planned in the process. **The key to quality control is self-control.** Self-control occurs when people have a system that lets them know their quality goals, know their performance against those goals, and have a means for adjusting the process (see Group Empowerment).

3. Quality Improvement

Improve competitiveness and reduce quality deficiencies. There must be clear responsibility for improvement. Top management must be fully involved through personal participation on project teams. Statements of intent are not enough. Management must do everything possible to avoid the perception that this will be just another project.

Quality improvement occurs on an incremental, project-by-project basis. Those organizations that wait for a major breakthrough will be overtaken by an organization that has hundreds of small improvement processes with full employee involvement. Everyone must become involved in discovering causes, identifying specific improvement projects, and working to improve quality.[9]

A Quality Council is comprised of upper management membership. The main job of these key managers is to establish an infrastructure for continuous improvement.

Essential leadership tasks:

- Include quality goals in the business plan

- Serve on quality council

- Serve on project teams

- Develop procedures for selecting improvement projects

- Approve strategic quality goals

- Allocate resources for teams and for improvement efforts

- Publish results

- Newsletters

- Give recognition

- Revise merit system

Managing for Quality: Details

Quality Management

Quality management is the way by which we achieve quality: quality planning, control, and improvement. The role of upper management is to serve on the Quality Council, establish goals, provide resources, review progress, give recognition, revise the reward system, serve on project teams, and recognize and deal with employee apprehension.

If employees feel that their jobs might be eliminated, reduce this conflict by stating that "…no employee will lose employment as a direct result of his or her involvement in a Quality Improvement effort." Otherwise, people will be reluctant to serve on Quality Improvement Teams (QITs).

Like Deming, and unlike Crosby, Juran dislikes exhortations and empty slogans. He distinguishes between cheerleading and leading, and, like both Deming and Crosby, he believes that management commitment and involvement are critical to the successful transformation of the organization.

In fact, Juran's advice to the Japanese back in 1954 was to focus on the management-controllable problems first, which they did, with very impressive results. As each problem area was addressed, the problem-solving process moved down the hierarchy on a layer-by-layer basis. About 10 years later, when most of the major management-controllable problems had been dealt with, it was time for the workers to address the remaining problems, which they were now capable of tackling.

Thus was born the quality circles movement in Japan. As conceived by Professor Kauro Ishikawa, the final management-controllable problem to be tackled was motivating the work force, and worker involvement in problem-solving teams was seen as an attractive motivational concept.[10]

Juran believes that the Quality Council is the key element in the organization's infrastructure. As quality improvement occurs on a project-by-project basis, teams should be organized by the council for specific quality improvement projects. He feels that a council member should sponsor each improvement project.

The quality council should meet on a regular basis to:

■ Approve department quality goals

■ Develop a plan for meeting quality goals

■ Evaluate quality performance

When planning for quality, statements such as "Quality has top priority" are meaningless. No one, including top management, takes these statements seriously unless they are accompanied by an action plan which includes a budget. Quality planning is never easy. It takes several years to establish quality improvement as a continuing, integral part of the operation of the organization.

Timetable for installing continuous quality improvement:

Activity	Months
Study of alternatives and decision to commit to annual quality improvement	6
Select test site, conduct pilot test (including training)	12
Evaluation of test site results, revision of approach, decision to scale up	6
Scale up across organization, and merge into business plan	24

Quality Control

Quality control is the managerial process consisting of evaluating actual performance, comparing actual performance to goals, and taking action on the difference. The feedback loop functions by using sensors (market surveys) to monitor attitudes and report back to an umpire. At the worker level, use technological-type sensors, where controls are aimed at the features of the product and process set out in the procedures manuals. At the managerial level, broad market feedback is needed to deal with broad issues of competitiveness and customer needs.

Self-control of quality occurs when the employee can make corrections to the system in order to bring the system into conformity. Self-control is a form of process ownership that responds to the basic human desire to control one's surroundings. It is absolutely necessary for motivation.

To have self-control, a person must have:

■ A means of knowing what the goals are (published standards)

■ A means of measuring and interpreting performance

■ A means of changing the process to bring it into conformance

It is risky for management to hold workers responsible for quality. What is required is recognition of the concept of controllability. Each feature of a product or process becomes a control subject—a center around which the feedback loop is built based on a sensor.

Effective Quality Measurement Requires:

■ A unit of measure (quality feature that permits evaluation)

■ A sensor (a measuring instrument) that carries out the evaluation
If a sensor to monitor a quality feature does not exist, then a project improvement team should be assigned the responsibility of developing such a sensor.

Planners must develop a means for employees to be able to adjust the process so that it conforms with goals:

■ Key product/process features must be known

■ Provide a means for adjusting the process setting

■ Predictable relationship between the amount of change in the process setting and level of effect on the product feature

■ Planners must understand natural process variability

Planners must acquire an in-depth knowledge of the relationship between process variables and the organization results. They must provide employees with reasonable performance goals and with process adjustment capability. Although Statistical Process Control (SPC) charts can be used, the statistical tool is **not** an end in itself. The important thing is for a project team to identify which projects to tackle, assign clear responsibility, and provide any resources needed.

Topics to consider when implementing self-control:

■ System for employees to communicate their views to management

■ System for management to keep employees informed of possible changes to the process they own before the changes are made

■ Training that explains the why as well as the how of doing something

■ Stress quality in the employment interview

■ Supervision that practices quality management

■ Supervision that merges employees into the planning process

---

An organization's products and services must provide customer satisfaction. A list of general quality goals is only a wish list. Subdivide the goals into specific, detailed goals for bite-size projects.

Vested interests that often prevent implementing self-control:

■ Managers lose their prerogatives about the time employees spend on projects versus time spent producing

■ Staff specialists face competition in planning and analysis

■ Employees are concerned with the impact of quality improvements on job security and are concerned about rewards for extra work

Juran summarizes several perceptual errors made by management regarding quality.

Errors in the perception of quality:

■ The work force is mainly responsible for the firm's quality problems.

■ Workers could do good quality work but lack the motivation to do so.

■ Workers are not in a state of self-control and therefore cannot produce good work.

■ Quality will get top priority if upper management so decrees. This is not true. Fundamental changes are needed in the way management conducts business. For example, all organizations should be involved in goal setting, planning to meet goals, resource allocation, measures of quality, progress reviews, and rewards based on meeting or exceeding quality goals.

■ To change people's behavior, it is first necessary to change their attitudes. Actually, if behavior is changed, then attitudes will change. For example, managers who have been required to serve on quality improvement teams exhibit greater receptivity to quality improvements.

See Joseph M. Juran, *Juran on Leadership for Quality: An Executive Handbook* (New York: The Free Press), 1989, 376 pp.

Exercise 4

Juran's Audit

Behavioral objectives:

Please change your behavior in this exercise to improve your ability to move the team forward. Do not fall into the common trap of simply analyzing what others are doing. Seek out opportunities to positively reinforce comments and actions of members that assist the team.

Time limit:

40 minutes

Instructions:

Get together in your assigned team and appoint a team member who has not previously served as a team leader. The leader is to guide the team in selecting an organization for a Juran audit. The leader is to make a specific point of calling on a "quiet" team member by name. This member is to make every effort to contribute in a way that moves the discussion forward.

After selecting an organization, each team member is to spend ten minutes and privately write down what he or she feels are the organization's three strongest and three weakest points. (If detailed knowledge of management teams or worker teams is available, then identify what Juran would think about the teams.) After writing down your ideas, get back together in your team.

Exercise 4

Juran's Organizational Audit Results

Three strongest points:

1.

2.

3.

Three weakest points:

1.

2.

3.

What is the main factor where Deming, Crosby, and Juran would differ?
Why?

Detach at perforation

Exercise 4

The team leader should try to reach a general agreement on what Juran would say were the organization's three weakest and three strongest points. Try to identify where Juran's analysis would differ from Deming's and Crosby's analyses. If there is sufficient time, try to reach a general agreement on what Juran would say regarding:

1. The organization's use of its human resources

2. The role of management

3. How the organization goes about reducing variations in the processes that produce goods and services

4. The methods used by the organization to continuously improve the quality of its goods and services

Exercise 4

5. Suppose Deming, Crosby, and Juran were addressing the executive board of the organization you selected. (This board is comprised of the president, chief executive officer, and three executive vice-presidents.)

■ Which of these contributors' philosophies would be easiest for the executive board to embrace? Why?

■ Which philosophy would be most difficult for them to embrace? Why?

Detach at perforation

Endnotes

1. Early studies by Elton Mayo are contained in *The Human Problems of Industrial Civilization* (New York: Macmillan, 1933), *The Social Problems of an Industrial Civilization* (Cambridge, Mass.: Harvard University Press, 1946), and *The Political Problems of an Industrial Civilization* (Cambridge, Mass.: Harvard University Press, 1947).

2. Notes from *A New Role for the Work Group,* by Maxine Bucklow (Chicago: University of Chicago Press, 1973); also selections from the features of a successful group by Clovis Shepard, published as *Small Groups: Some Sociological Perspectives* (San Francisco: Chandler Publishing, 1964).

3. Suggested readings: W.G. Bennis, "A New Role for the Behavioral Sciences: Effecting Organizational Change," *Administrative Science Quarterly,* Vol. 8, pp. 125–165, 1963; L.P. Bradford, J.R. Gibb, and K.P. Benne, *T-Group Theory and the Laboratory Method* (New York: John Wiley), 1964; C. Argyis, *Interpersonal Competence and Organizational Effectiveness* (New York: Dorsey Press), 1962 and *Personality and Organization* (New York: Harper and Row), 1957; R.R. Blake and J.S. Mouton, "The Developing Revolution in Management Practices," *American Society of Training Directors Journal,* Vol. 16, pp. 29–52, 1962 and *Group Dynamics Key to Decision Making* (Houston: Gulf Publishing), 1961; H.R. Shepard and R.R. Blake, "Changing Behavior Through Cognitive Maps," *Human Organization,* Vol. 21, pp. 88–96, 1962.

4. R.R. Blake, J.S. Mouton, L.L. Barnes, and L.E. Greiner, "Breakthrough in Organization Development," *Harvard Business Review,* Vol. 42, pp. 133–155, 1964; R.R. Blake and J.S. Mouton, *The Managerial Grid* (Houston: Gulf Publishing), 1964.

5. Over the years, Dr. Deming has gradually focused his teachings into a body of knowledge that is epitomized by his "Theory of Profound Knowledge," which has at its core a knowledge of statistics. In his apartment in New York City, a sign above his study door read, "In God we trust; all others must bring data." And data to Deming meant statistics.

6. Dr. Deming, *Out of Crisis* (Cambridge, Mass.: MIT Center for Advanced Engineering), 1991.

7. Dr. William Scherkenback, in his work "Deming's Road to Continuous Improvement," tells a story about Bud Chicoine, when he was Vice President for Purchasing at Ford. Bill commented to Dr. Deming, "I know what I told our buyers; I do not know what they heard." Ford uses the American Supplier Institute (ASI) to monitor their hearing and supplier teams were formed to improve their system of feedback.

8. See Crosby's book, *Quality Is Free* (New York: New American Library, 1979).

9. During the early 1980s Florida Power and Light (FPL) worked very closely with Dr. Juran in the creation of its award-winning team program, which at its peak consisted of almost 2000 active teams in operation. When FPL applied for the Deming prize in 1987–88, Dr. Deming made it known that he was not in favor of the FPL Juran-based approach to teams. Deming viewed these teams as "parallel organizational entities" which co-existed alongside the regular organization and operated for the most part outside the system.

   The rivalry between the gurus was apparent, and on the day that FPL won the Deming prize, Frank Voehl and Mary Walton called him to inform him of the achievement, to which he replied: "So, they're pupils of Juran's, not mine." Apparently, loyalty to one's guru was an esteemed virtue, and FPL did not rate high on Dr. Deming's list because of Juran's heavy influence, especially in the area of teams.

10. In his work entitled *Achieve Total Quality,* author David Hutchins spells out in detail the typical evolution of Total Quality in most organizations that are considered to be successful followers of the Juran method. He points out that intensive use of project teams at the managerial level followed by extensive development and support of the quality circle/worker teams, along with a meaningful suggestion system, are the backbone of the process.

Chapter 3

Empowerment

Empowerment is a relatively new term in the management literature, but its counterpart—authority—has been around for centuries. The dictionary definition of empowerment is "to invest with power, especially legal power or authority." Empowerment is synonymous with authority.

The Xerox Corporation has developed a more practical working definition of empowerment:

> An organizational state where people are aligned with the business direction and understand their performance boundaries, thus enabling them to take responsibility and ownership for: seeking improvements, identifying the best course of action, and initiating the necessary steps to satisfy customer requirements.[1]

Xerox believes that this definition is important because it helps both individuals and teams answer the question, "What am I empowered to do?" The definition also helps focus everyone's role on the fundamental objective of every organization: to achieve and maintain 100% customer satisfaction. Note that the heart of empowerment is the sharing of power among the organizational teams, and in turn the teams must take responsibility for their actions.

One study of companies using teams[2] found that teams had:

■ Greater productivity

■ More effective use of resources

■ Better problem-solving success

In addition, teams produced better quality products and services. This was not surprising, because teams have often been found to produce higher quality products in less time than more traditional groups operating in a hierarchical structure. Not only are products produced better, but service quality is enhanced.[2,3] In preparing for team development, the team must learn how to establish work priorities, solve problems without the assistance of supervision, and improve the interpersonal process of the group.

Team development is an ongoing process, not a single event. People who want to "get away for a while and do team building" have an incorrect notion of what team building is all about.[3] The program of team building is designed to alter the way an integrated unit functions together.

Do not assume that simply calling a group of employees a team means they will automatically function as a team and the organization will reap the benefits. In reality, it just does not happen that way. A group must go through a change process to begin functioning as a team. Training will be needed to develop self-awareness and decision-making ability. In addition, assistance will be needed in establishing a mission (direction) for the team and in identifying training needs.[4]

Empowerment is a state of mind, as well as the result of organizational practices. Empowerment stems from both the policies supported by management and from the individual choices made by group members. To feel empowered means that the individual is a member of a team in every sense, and the individual:

■ Takes responsibility for his or her situation

■ Has a vision of something worthwhile (i.e., a purpose for the work he or she does)

■ Makes a commitment to achieving that purpose

When a manager asks people to take responsibility for their own actions and their own unit (team), then the manager must be willing to give up some of his or her control. In doing so, a setting is created

Team Development

I. Traditional Hierarchy

II. Individual Power Sharing

III. Group Power Sharing

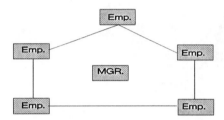

IV. Group/Team Development

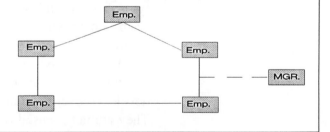

where people put energy, excitement, and motivation into their work. Thus, empowering others takes time, skill, and the commitment of managers. The manager no longer directly intervenes in the everyday running of the group or in the assignment of tasks. The employees perform these activities.

Has something like the situation above ever happened to you? This type of runaround is not the fault of the student advising department. Each department involved in the process (student advising, student records, registrar, finance, bookstore, public safety, and student affairs) looks at its small portion of the process and probably feels it is efficient. These departments are part of a bureaucracy which has developed over time and is focused inward on departmental concerns. They are not focused on the needs of the customers.

Hence the customer's needs are not being met. A team approach is required to evaluate this condition, cut through the red tape, and empower the student advising office to do its job: advise students with a minimum of hassle.

Continuous Quality Improvement (CQI) is a philosophy that involves the sharing of power with employees working in empowered teams. It is getting everyone in the firm—management, employees, and support services—to focus on the consumer.

An effective quality improvement effort requires that everyone buys into the concept. That is, an environment must be created where employees **want** to do a better job, instead of being required to do better. This is not as difficult to accomplish as it might sound. People basically want to do a good or better job and will appreciate the opportunity to do so.

Returning to our student advising example, if the advisor is empowered, what about the people who work in the support departments (student records, registrar, finance, bookstore, public safety, student affairs)? Will they lose power?

Not everyone gains when power is shared. The organization will inevitably be realigned to reflect the changing priorities. Management in some departments will most likely lose power, and there is a natural tendency to fight any loss of power and prestige. The power of a manager is generally related to the number of employees in the department. All things being equal, the higher the head count, the higher the power, and the greater the salary of the managerial position.

Sure, empowered employees will have to change their method of doing business. Frequently, however, one result in an empowered organization is that there is less need for middle management. It is therefore middle managers who frequently have the most to lose with empowerment because they must learn new leadership skills.

Meaningful Quality

For quality to be a personal and an organizational value:

- It must be chosen freely

- It must be chosen from alternatives

- It must be acted upon by the person and the organization

- It must help people achieve their potential and help the organization achieve its potential

- It must be publicly affirmed by the person and the organization

---

In addition to playing a "numbers game," managers have traditionally increased their power through controls. Many a manager's job is a "signature cycle" or a "must obtain approval from" type of position. These delays are not allowed in an empowered organization. However, the president cannot simply issue an administrative memo directing the organization to adopt CQI. A CQI philosophy requires a change in the basic way business is conducted.

Changes required for CQI:

Issues	Change from:	Change to:
Defects	Inevitable	Zero defects
Training	Cost	Investment
Change	Resisted	Way of life
Time horizon	Short term	Long term
Customers	Take it or leave it	Satisfaction
Vendors	Price	Price and quality
Performance	Cost and schedule	Customer requirements
Information flow	Vertical	Horizontal and vertical
Performance goals	Standards	Better than yesterday
Management role	Enforcer	Coach

Due to the behavioral changes that are needed, it takes years to develop empowered teams in organizations. Management has to be truly willing to share meaningful power with the team, and the team has to be responsible enough to effectively utilize this power. Both conditions must be met, and both management and the teams must trust each other to function effectively.

Empowered firms:

■ Accomplish work through independent teams

■ Foster an environment that develops, encourages, and rewards empowered people and teams

■ Encourage people to build social and technical skills

■ Align personal and organizational goals and see that people understand their roles

■ Exhibit a high level of individual and team self-management

■ Participate in work design, set direction, and resolve problems

■ Provide people with the information they need—without asking

---

An empowered firm accomplishes work through independent teams. Meaningful power is delegated to these teams to perform their work without the customary signature cycles, approval cycles, or waiting for other departments to perform their tasks.

Team Empowerment

Team responsibilities:

69%	Safety and housekeeping
58	Assign task to members
53	Work with internal customers
46	Stop work for quality issues
45	Routine equipment maintenance
44	Vacation scheduling
42	Process improvements
38	Select work methods
34	External customers
33	Determine training needs
29	Set production goals

Team empowerment often begins with small steps. Once an effective team is formed, with members who can work with one another, the team members should agree that they will be responsible for certain tasks.

Team Empowerment

Shared responsibilities:

54%   Select work methods

53   Determine training methods

51   Process improvements

49   Set production goals

44   Individual performance problems

44   Routine equipment maintenance

44   External customers

Supervisor responsibilities:

70%   Compensation decisions

55   Prepare and manage budgets

46   Performance appraisals

41   Individual performance problems

Some tasks should be shared with supervisors. That is, the team accepts supervisory input as guidance. Other tasks, such as compensation decisions, are often left for supervisors to perform.

Barriers to success:

■ Personnel issues

■ Supervisor resistance

■ Transfer of power to teams

■ Misalignment—compensation and team structure

■ Difficulty with team members and supervisors in new roles

See Kast and Laughlin, "Views on Self-Directed Workteams," *Journal for Quality and Participation,* pp. 48–51, December 1990.

However, it won't be easy. There are natural barriers to success. People who are used to working alone will now have to function together as a team. Supervisors who use to control activities will have to change to more of a coaching style of leadership.

Empowered teams must have a process of self-control, where the team assumes responsibility for its performance. A good way of visualizing this is in terms of "Results Displayed," where the team reports (charts) a critical success factor.

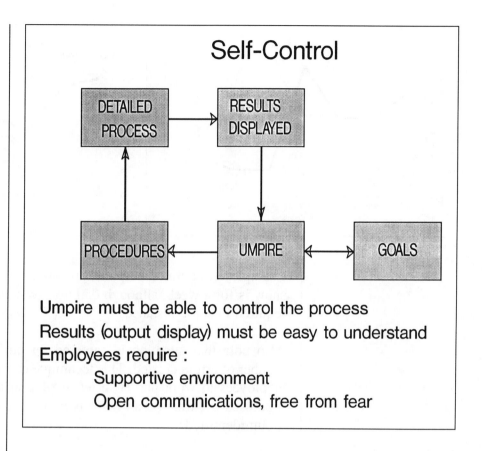

Self-Control

DETAILED PROCESS → RESULTS DISPLAYED

PROCEDURES ← UMPIRE ↔ GOALS

Umpire must be able to control the process
Results (output display) must be easy to understand
Employees require :
    Supportive environment
    Open communications, free from fear

Management will have to assist the group in its first step toward empowerment, which is to get control of their output. Without knowledge of their output quality levels, groups cannot correct their actions when needed.

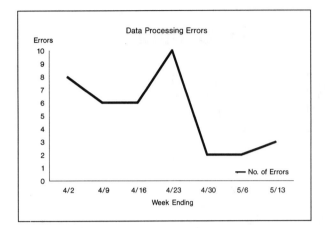

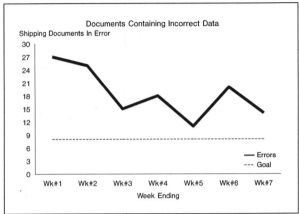

Examples of common output charts are shown here. The time period show is for a week, although daily or even hourly tracking might be required in some instances.

Also note that attention is centered on quality issues, such as the number of errors created. This technique cannot be used to encourage employees to work harder in terms of charting the number of units processed per time period. Nor is individual performance within the group identified.

The objective of charting group output on a critical quality factor is to ensure that team members are aware of their quality levels.

When designing a beginning group empowerment system, concentrate on how the data will be captured (recorded). Inevitably this will require a special form. This is typically the responsibility of an employee who is called the umpire. This function is rotated among all employees in the group, often on a monthly basis.

The empowerment comes about by asking the umpire to discuss what happened in a group meeting with the employees involved present. The point is not to highlight blame, but instead to openly discuss the process and what can be done to improve it.

Exercise 5

What Is Empowerment?

Behavioral objectives:

1. To become aware of the effect you have on the team, and to assist the leader in obtaining balanced contributions from all team members. Practice positive reinforcement on a team member whose comments and actions assist the team.

2. To develop an understanding of what empowerment means. What does a team do when it is empowered?

Time limit:

25 minutes

Instructions:

Appoint a new team leader to coordinate the team. Then spend five minutes answering the following questions on team empowerment. When answering this questionnaire, assume that you are working at the headquarters of a 100-year-old insurance corporation. The company employs 1600 people in its headquarters, and the chief executive has developed empowered teams.

After answering the questions, get back together in your team and try to reach a consensus on the answers.

Exercise 5

Empowerment							

IN MY OPINION:	Strongly Disagree					Strongly Agree	
1. Empowered teams are used for tasks such as streamlining claims payments	1	2	3	4	5	6	7
2. Empowered teams cut across traditional functional lines	1	2	3	4	5	6	7
3. Empowered teams are welcomed by department managers	1	2	3	4	5	6	7
4. Team members must obtain approval from department management committing departmental resources	1	2	3	4	5	6	7
5. Team members should keep their department management in touch with the various actions the empowered team is considering	1	2	3	4	5	6	7
6. Empowered teams should report progress on a regular basis to the executive who created the team	1	2	3	4	5	6	7
7. Empowered teams should be permitted to elicit assistance from any department, even from departments that do not have a representative on the team	1	2	3	4	5	6	7

Detach at perforation

Exercise 6

Team Process Control

Behavioral objectives:

To understand that empowerment requires team members to assume responsibility for their output quality. This means that the team must gain control of its portion of the production process.

Empowerment requires that all team members have a high commitment to quality. Team members do not have to wait for management to suggest changes. Changes are made as required so that output is constantly of high quality.

Time limit:

25 minutes

Instructions:

Get together in your team and create a system that will enable a small team of empowered employees to identify when a process is out of control. The small group of employees (i.e., the team that will use the process) must be able to report a key quality output of the process and make adjustments when they are needed to bring the process in control.

Exercise 6

Concentrate on developing a sketch of the Results Displayed:

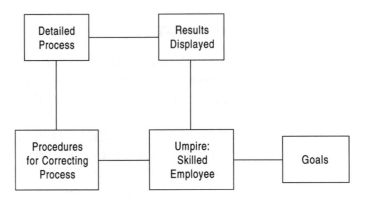

The output of an actual detailed process should be shown on an easy-to-read bulletin board. The umpire (group leader) observes the results displayed (the output) and makes adjustments to the process via written procedures so that the goals are met.

Avoid the following common errors in your empowerment application:

An attempt to eliminate a problem	Establish a continuous process whereby employees can identify when an out-of-control condition occurs. Self-control is the key to CQI!
A complex, broadly defined process	The process must be a detailed sub-process that is well defined and fully understood.
Management involvement	Should be none.
Complex goals	If the goals are not simple and easy to understand, how can employees make corrections?
Broad phrases	Be very specific.
Complex output display	Display must be simple.

Detach at perforation

Endnotes

1. Source: The Xerox Corporate Management Institute.

2. G.M. Parker, *Team Players and Teamwork* (San Francisco: Jossey-Bass), 1990.

3. W.G. Dyer, *Team Building,* 2nd ed. (Reading, Mass.: Addison-Wesley), 1987.

4. Robert Hughes, "Stepping Stones for Self-Directed Work Teams," *Training,* Vol. 28(2), p. 44, Dec. 1991.

Chapter 4

Supportive Team Cultures

Removing managerial controls and the transference of power is at the core of empowerment. The group members should not feel they have to obtain approval for everything they do. Empowering a team means that the manager has removed the barriers that prevent the expression of individual power.[1] The team members must be able to exercise self-judgment and begin to develop an understanding of what needs to be done, rather than being told what to do.

The manager's attitude and actions are important in creating the confidence, courage, and commitment that people need to act with responsible freedom. Of course, general guidelines will have to be established, but these guidelines should not be treated as procedures (or laws). The organizational culture should take over and provide a vision of what the organization is trying to accomplish. The culture also supports the development of skills so that people are equipped to do what needs to be done. Finally, the culture provides payoffs, both emotionally and materially, so that people want to "go the extra mile." In a culturally diverse work force, less than effective communication can compromise the final team results. The same words, tones, and gestures often have different meanings. Therefore, team members must learn to be aware of individual and cultural differences, avoid stereotyping, and restate what others have said to clarify the message.

A Variety of Team-Player Styles

Sound teamwork is based upon an effective mix of people, and each person should realize the unique contribution he or she can make to the team. An employee is thus encouraged to feel empowered in terms of exercising judgment and feeling comfortable with his or her role and contribution to the team. Each of us has the capacity to be an effective team player and to make a positive contribution to the team. For example, you might be willing to learn a new system and take on an additional responsibility that is needed by the team. Another person might help by encouraging some of the quieter people to get involved in the discussions or by using humor to reduce tension in the group.

Another team member may recommend that the team develop goals and an action plan. Someone else may insist that the team take a critical look at one of its key projects. All these examples represent contributions to the team, either directly to the product or service being produced or indirectly in terms of moving the team forward.

Another way to view these valuable differences members bring to a team is in terms of problem-solving styles. An effective team needs both creative and empirical thinkers. That is, if we all thought alike, the team would neither be creative nor have the ability to follow through on ideas.

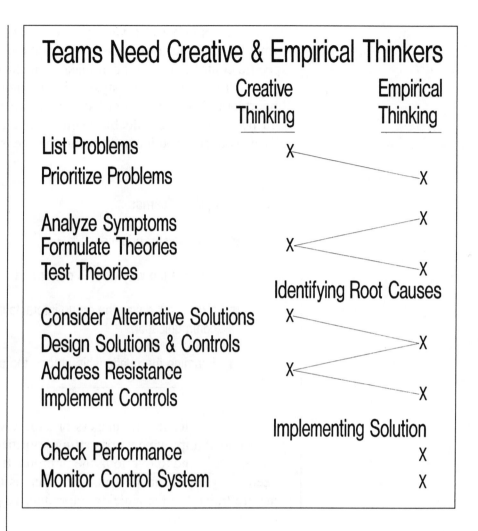

Team players come in a variety of uniforms and with varied equipment. Develop an awareness of your style, your strengths, and the specific contributions you can make to a team effort. Be flexible and open to "fine-tuning" your style of interacting with the team. It is also important to become a better listener. If you can accomplish this, you will become a more valuable team member, particularly if you can change your contribution to meet varying needs as the situation changes.

Analyzing Teams:

■ Set goals or priorities

■ Analyze the way work is performed

■ Examine the way the group interacts in decision making and communication

■ Examine the relationship among the people doing the work

Organizational leaders (managers or supervisors) often see the problem as one of improving work, setting priorities, and improving performance. They tend to overlook the unproductive interrelationships between the team members. Outsiders such as teachers and facilitators, who are trained in recognizing unproductive group dynamics, can be very helpful here.

Team development should begin with a strong desire to improve some basic output or process that is interfering with achievement of organizational goals. The issue is how to install these characteristics in a group that does not already possess them. There are several ways of accomplishing this. Using an outside facilitator is perhaps the easiest and quickest way to implement changes. An outside facilitator is viewed as a neutral, non-political person who has no hidden agenda.

A multi-phased approach is required to develop a team. We will review these phases (Phases II to V are discussed in Chapter 5) and then begin the team-building exercises.

Phase I	Initial group meeting
Phase II	Discussion of barriers and gateways
Phase III	Teams versus groups
Phase IV	Team development
Phase V	Reinforcement

Phase I: Initial Group Meeting

The objective of the first group meeting is to begin the process of developing trust and a working relationship with the team members. The team will have to appoint an initial leader (this role will be rotated), and the leader might well begin the discussion by explaining the main objective: to get the group working together as a team. One way to accomplish this is to encourage group members to share their feelings about the group itself. Included in this discussion would be the general characteristics of an effective team.

It is difficult for teams to hold effective meetings if one or more members attempt to control the team by dominating the discussion, talking excessively, judging what others say, or not actively participating in the group. It is the responsibility of the team members to be aware that such activities can occur and to openly discuss what is happening in the group.

Sample Team Rules

One of the most important topics for discussion in the initial group meeting is the establishment of written rules governing the responsibilities of team membership. Do not think that being a team member is easy just because a superior does not define what is to be done. Typical team rules include several factors. For example, it is a reality of life that some team members will offer excuses as to why they missed or cannot attend a team meeting. This should be dealt with openly: absenteeism will not be tolerated.

It is not advisable to "carry" a team member who is not contributing to the team. Experience has shown that this is a waste of time beyond any possible contribution the individual could make. Take the initiative and drop from the team any members who do not contribute.

Sample Team Rules:

■ Regular meetings will be determined by team members.

■ Four team members must be present for a meeting, which will constitute a quorum. The meeting will start and end on time, and members should be prepared to participate.

■ If a member misses more than two unexcused team meetings, that member is dropped from the team.

■ A member may be dropped from a team for failing to attend meetings or for failing to actively contribute to the team.

■ A vote of 75% or more of the team is needed to drop a member from a team. (This 75% vote does not including the member to be removed.) The instructor/facilitator is to be notified of the name of the team member(s) who is no longer on the team and the reason he or she was removed from the team.

■ Team members must be committed to attending all meetings. An effort should be made to accommodate the varying schedules of team members. However, if a member cannot attend due to work or any other reason, that member is not contributing to the team and will be dropped from the team.

Sample Team Rules (continued):

■ The last ten minutes of each meeting will be used to critique the performance of team members and prepare the agenda for the next team meeting.

■ Service roles, including team leader, recorder, and observer, will be determined by team members. Assignment of these roles is to rotate and is to be determined at the end of each meeting.

■ The designated recorder will record minutes of the meeting and file them in a Master Minutes Book, which will be maintained for the team. Also, the Observer's Recording Form (to be discussed) **must** be completed for each meeting and filed in the Master Minutes Book (held by a designed team member).

■ This minutes book must be turned in to the instructor/facilitator when designated for review. In addition, the minutes book must accompany the final QI project.

■ Prior to turning in the minutes book, each team member is to anonymously complete a Peer Evaluation Form, which is turned into the instructor/facilitator.

Reaching a Consensus

When working together as a team, decisions should be made by consensus after issues have been discussed. Do not simply force a vote and go with the majority. During discussions, conflict in the form of disagreement is natural, and these differences can bring about high-quality, creative solutions to problems. However, it is important that conflict be directed toward substantive issues and not personalities. As a team member, it is your right to disagree with what is said. When voicing your disagreement, however, avoid letting personalities enter into the discussion, in the form of subtle put-downs and innuendos, when the discussion strays from the issues involved.

Voicing disagreement is not enough, however. As a team member, you should assist in developing meaningful alternatives. You do not have to agree with others who may criticize your ideas, but you do have to accept the reality that the person offering the criticism is serious. The objective is to deal constructively with the situation by discussing issues and moving the team forward in seeking a solution.

Several things can be done to improve the effectiveness of a meeting, beginning with the concept of voting. Voting in a group is considered to be a democratic practice; after all, we are doing what the majority wants. However, the nature of voting means that someone must lose. The losing party has not bought into the proposal and does not feel obligated to implement the proposal. Hence, the beginning point for team development is to avoid voting and instead reach a consensus on issues.

Consensus is a general understanding. It does not imply unanimous or complete agreement with a proposal. It does, however, imply that the members feel that the proposal discussed is the most acceptable course of action in terms of the task to be accomplished. Reaching a consensus takes more time than voting, yet it is essential in order to encourage everyone to voice what is on their mind and express their feelings. This is particularly important in meetings where the decisions made have to be implemented. At this point, it will be helpful to review Table 1, Characteristics of an Effective Team, in Chapter 1. Note that most of the points in the table deal with consensus building.

Endnote

1. Jerry Harvey in 1974 first developed the notion of the "Abilene Paradox," which observed that people often engage in dysfunctional and ineffective behavior. The antidote, according to Murrell in the *Organization Development Journal* (pp. 47–52, Fall 1992) may be empowered teams operating on three operating assumptions: trust, assertion, and clarity of goals and roles.

Exercise 7

Salesman Problem

Behavioral objectives:

To develop skills in reaching a team consensus.

Time limit:

30 minutes

Instructions:

Get together in your team and appoint a team leader. Then privately read the following mini-case on a problem that was encountered with Tom, a salesperson at Thompson Industries. What do you think the sales manager, Ms. Joyce Franks, should do? Be specific and state two proposed courses of action in the space provided. Be prepared to support your proposed courses of action.

You have eight minutes to read the case and record your two suggested courses of action. Then meet together in your assigned team and try to reach a consensus on the action that Ms. Franks should undertake. The team **must** come up with no more than three specific action items, which should be proposed in the order in which they should be undertaken.

When attempting to reach consensus, remember:

■ No voting. You are trying to reach a general agreement that everyone can live with.

■ Present your ideas, but avoid arguing in order to "win" as an individual.

■ Each team member is responsible for monitoring interactions and discussing the process when the team becomes ineffective.

Exercise 7

Mini-Case

For several months, Ms. Joyce Franks, sales manager at Thompson Industries, has been concerned that Mr. Tom Jones, one of the salesmen, has not been following up on existing accounts. She previously told Tom about complaints she received and that he must pay more attention to his accounts. She suspects that he has done nothing.

It isn't that Tom is a bad salesman; in fact, he brings in as many new accounts as anyone else on the staff. He loves to put on a "show" when courting potential new customers, including driving them to dinner in a limousine, providing them with theater tickets, and even catering lunch at the client's firm.

However, Ajax Industries, a very large account that Tom landed last year, has complained twice that they were not aware of product price changes. Now their Purchasing Manager is threatening to cancel because a product was phased out without informing them of a substitute.

Your proposed course of action:

1.

2.

Detach at perforation

Exercise 8

Secretarial Problem

Behavioral objectives:

To refine our skills in reaching a team consensus.

Time limit:

20 minutes

Instructions:

Appoint a new team leader to coordinate your input. You have five minutes to privately read the mini-case on a problem that was encountered with Sue, a secretary with Goodfellow Hospital. Using the form provided, record your answer as to what you think her manager, Ms. Alice Manner, should do. Be specific and state two proposed courses of action in the space provided. Be prepared to support your proposed courses of action.

Then meet together in your assigned team and try to reach a consensus on the action that Ms. Manner should undertake. The team **must** come up with no more than three specific action items, which should be proposed in the order in which they should be undertaken.

Exercise 8

Mini-Case

Sue has been a good worker at Goodfellow Hospital for the past four years, and she seems to think that she is destined for a top administrative position. The problem is that she only received a satisfactory performance evaluation during her last performance review, whereas previously she had consistently received the higher rating of outstanding. It was pointed out that she returns late from lunch, takes hour-long personal phone calls, and tends to blow events out of proportion.

When her manager, Ms. Manner, pointed out these facts in a discussion of the performance review, Sue became very argumentative and then angry. Since then, her performance has deteriorated further.

Your proposed course of action:

1.

2.

Chapter 5

Team-Building Phases

The concept of team-building phases was introduced in Chapter 4, although only the first phase, the initial group meeting, was discussed. The initial phase is the foundation for empowerment, where people learn how to work together in teams.

Organizations will want to go into greater depth in developing their teams. One way to get the teams to develop themselves is to ask members to anonymously answer a questionnaire that focuses on:

Personal goals	What keeps you, personally, from doing the kind of job you would like to do?
Organizational potential	What things does the organization do best?
Organizational improvement	What could be done to improve the organization?

Responses to these questions are collected and summarized by the instructor/facilitator for later feedback to the group.

Phase II:
Discussion of Barriers and Gateways[1]

After the responses are summarized, the leader/facilitator should make the summaries available to the group and ask the members how they feel about the issues identified. The objective is to develop an atmosphere where people feel comfortable "putting items on the table." Although solutions would be nice, that is not the primary purpose of discussions of barriers and gateways. The group is trying to learn a process whereby members can identify areas where improvements can be made. Group ownership is encouraged through this process of participation in group ideas.

Phase III:
Teams versus Groups

This phase involves an examination of the characteristics of teams versus groups. A group is a collection of individuals who are in an interdependent relationship with one another. A team goes beyond that, in that members are encouraged to share in the ownership of the team's function and direction. Each member will then share in the ownership of the team's functions and direction.

Team	Versus	Group
Decisions made by consensus with all inputs heard and valued		Groups tend to have majority and minority opinions
Disagreements are carefully examined and resolution is sought		Criticism tends to be destructive and disagreements are not effectively dealt with
Objectives are well understood and accepted by the team		Group members do not necessarily accept common objectives
Free expression of ideas occurs and others listen to what is said		Personal feelings are hidden
Self examination of how the group is functioning frequently occurs		Discussions are avoided regarding how the group is functioning
Roles are understood by all members		Individuals tend to protect their role and their niche in the group
Shared leadership occurs on an as-needed basis		Leadership is appointed

To assist in the development of a comprehensive team-building effort, the team members should discuss:

1. Team member responsibility

2. The team within the organization

3. The team and the individual

4. The team and the work performed

5. Team goals and objectives

Phase IV:
Team Development

Activities are undertaken to improve the operating effectiveness of the work team and its ability to resolve issues that arise as team members work together. An additional questionnaire would be used to examine how the team functions in five general areas.

1	**Environmental influences**	Impact on team performance due to policies, procedures, customers, etc.
2	**Goals**	How are team goals established?
3	**Roles**	Does everyone know what is expected of them?
4	**Processes**	Effectiveness of meetings, decision making, communication
5	**Interpersonal dynamics**	How team members work together and the impact on the team's effectiveness

Phase V: Reinforcement:
Energizing for Performance Improvement

There is a tendency for a newly formed team to become mired in detail. An outside person can often assist the team in obtaining an objective view as to how it is focused. Answers are sought to basic questions such as "where have we been" and "where are we going," to help the team identify areas where changes may be needed.

> ### Do Teams Really Need an Instructor/Facilitator?
>
> No, you do not need either an instructor or a facilitator, provided the group is willing to work together. In an organizational setting, often the Human Resources Department can provide a trained facilitator, who can be invaluable to the group. This person can make life easier, because he or she has been through the process before and knows the "stumbling blocks."

Summary

It is not difficult for management to start a CQI program. The difficulty lies in converting a "management program" into an ongoing process where quality improvements occur automatically. Quality improvement must be viewed as a journey, not a destination. This means a shift to facilitative leadership that exhibits the following characteristics:

1. Leading with vision

2. Becoming a learner

3. Focusing on process as well as outcome

4. Coaching and developing team members

5. Linking and connecting teams and organizational units

6. Knowledge of psychology and systems thinking

This is difficult to achieve because it requires leaders to assume new roles. In fact, not only will leaders be affected in the new culture, but new forms of labor will also be required. Shoshana Zuboff, in her book entitled *The Age of the Smart Machine,* discusses learning as a new form of labor, which is no longer a separate activity that occurs either before one enters the workplace or in a remote classroom setting. She feels that learning is at the heart of productive activity, and the facilitative leader must develop a climate in which team excellence and empowerment can flourish. Also, a facilitative leader helps the team develop a learning environment.

Selected Readings

Richard Beckhard and R.T. Harris, *Organizational Transitions,* 2nd ed. (Reading, Mass.: Addison-Wesley), 1987.

C.R. Bell, "Empowerment Is Not a Gift," *Training,* Vol. 28(12), p. 98, Dec. 1991.

Peter Block, *The Empowered Manager: Positive Political Skills at Work* (San Francisco: Jossey-Bass), 1987.

W.G. Dyer, *Team Building,* 2nd ed. (Reading, Mass.: Addison-Wesley), 1987.

Robert Hughes, "Stepping Stones for Self-Directed Work Teams," *Training,* Vol. 28(2), p. 44, Dec. 1991.

Douglas McGregor, *The Human Side of Enterprise* (New York: McGraw-Hill), 1960.

G.M. Parker, *Team Players and Teamwork* (San Francisco: Jossey-Bass), 1990.

Endnote

1. The concept of barriers and gateways is based on a technique called force-field analysis, where the forces for and against an idea can be analyzed, diagrammed, and evaluated in some type of quasi-scientific manner. As in one's work life, team members will not let go of their current "safe" behaviors until they feel they have something to grasp onto that will be secure. Teams can minimize resistance to change by making it safe for team members to try new behaviors. Teams and team members should analyze and learn from their failures as much as their successes, in order to increase their confidence and commitment.

Exercise 9

Written Team Rules

Behavioral objectives:

To be responsible for your own performance and for the performance of your team.

Time limit:

See your instructor for the completion time for this exercise.

Instructions:

Get together in your assigned team. Develop written rules governing what you will attempt to accomplish. Also include rules governing the behavior and performance of team members. These rules are to be agreed to in writing by all team members. One copy is given to the instructor/facilitator and a copy is retained by each team member.

Exercise 9

Written Team Rules

Detach at perforation

Exercise 10

Team Assessment

Behavioral objectives:

To provide the feedback that is necessary for teams to evaluate their performance.

Time limit:

20 minutes

Instructions:

Get together in your assigned team and elect a team leader, who will gather the answers to the questionnaires, summarize the responses, and report back to the team at the next meeting. This person should be someone who has not recently served in a leadership role.

Each team member, including the team leader, is to anonymously answer the questionnaire as an aid in assessing the team's performance. Please choose the number that best describes how you feel about each statement. The further away from the middle (4), the stronger your feeling about the statement. Turn your completed questionnaire in to the team leader.

Exercise 10

Team Assessment

IN MY OPINION:	Strongly Disagree						Strongly Agree
1. This was an effective meeting	1	2	3	4	5	6	7
2. I clearly understood the team goals for this meeting	1	2	3	4	5	6	7
3. The team stayed on track in working toward its goals	1	2	3	4	5	6	7
4. The team considered my contributions	1	2	3	4	5	6	7
5. I felt free to express my opinions and make a contribution to the group	1	2	3	4	5	6	7
6. Conversation was balanced among members	1	2	3	4	5	6	7
7. I was satisfied with this meeting	1	2	3	4	5	6	7

Detach at perforation

Peer Feedback

The discussion of empowered teams will continue in a moment, but let's not lose track of what we are trying to accomplish. We are learning how we think, work, and act together as a team. You will be asked to assume specific roles as a team member, and you will be asked to rotate assignment of those role. However, the hard part is learning how your behavior affects the team.

You will have to change your behavior to improve your effectiveness as a team member. Think about this statement. People typically attend meetings, voice comments, and feel they have made a contribution, but that's nonsense. Your contribution is not what you say or do, but instead how you are able to move the team forward. This is a difficult concept because we often think in terms of what we say or do, and not the effect our actions have on a team.

Try not to be defensive when group interactions are discussed, including your contribution to the team. Look at this process as a unique opportunity to learn methods to improve the effectiveness of your team. Once you learn the basic interaction skills, you should be able to continuously improve your ability to work as a member of a team. Exercises 11 and 12 include peer evaluation questions which deal with your effectiveness as a member of a team.

Do's and Don'ts When Giving Feedback

One of the most difficult tasks for a team member to perform is evaluating another member's contribution to the team, particularly when an actual grade is to be assigned. This evaluation must be as objective as possible, without introducing personalities into the evaluation.

Be specific when justifying the grade assigned to a team member. Avoid generalities or personal comments. Positive feedback is far more welcome than negative comments. Try to pick out one or two contributions the member made to the team.

A Few Do's and Don't When Giving Feedback

Do	Don't
Be positive and thank members for the specific contributions they made.	Say "everyone did a good job." (Identify what each specific individual did or did not contribute.)
Be specific when someone's actions hurt the team. Try to provide positive feedback: "I understand your strong feelings regarding the proposal, but we needed to reach a group consensus we all could live with."	Say "your constant complaining annoyed me." (Phrase the sentence objectively, and provide a specific example.)
Be clear. For example, if the issue was a failure to offer useful team input, state: "If you would have expressed your ideas on developing team rules more positively, I'm sure the group would have been more willing to include your suggestions."	Get involved in trivia such as, "Your failure to make eye contact decreases your effectiveness."

Disagreements in grading the contributions of team members are to be resolved by the team, if at all possible. If disagreements cannot be resolved by the team, then the facilitator–instructor should be consulted. More specific documentation will be available later in the form of a Master Minutes Book (containing the team minutes) and participant interaction forms (which are completed for each meeting) to back up any claims.

Exercise 11

General Peer Feedback

Behavioral objectives:

To provide the feedback that is necessary for individual team members to improve their performance.

Time limit:

20 minutes

Instructions:

Get together in your assigned team. Elect a team member to facilitate the peer feedback process in a manner which ensures that the respondents remain anonymous. This person should be someone who has not recently served in a team function.

Every team member is to participate in providing peer feedback on two other team members. (The data are not analyzed, nor does the facilitator participate in the evaluation.) The facilitator simply decides who is to analyze whom and ensures that the forms are distributed correctly.

Begin by completing the grid provided on the next page. Write the names of the team members on the left side of the grid. Then fill in the names of the **two** members who are assigned to analyze each team member. Ask the team members to open their books to the General Peer Feedback form. Then walk to where each person is seated and record the name of the team member who is being evaluated (i.e., each team member evaluates two other team members). After the evaluation is completed, pick up the forms and distribute them to the appropriate people.

Exercise 11

Peer Feedback Assignments		
Team Member	**Evaluated by:**	**Evaluated by:**

Detach at perforation

Exercise 11

General Peer Feedback

Answer the following questions to provide feedback to the team member indicated. Check the number that you believe represents the usual behavior of that team member. The farther away from the middle (4), the stronger the team member's behavior.

Name: _____

IN MY OPINION THIS PERSON:	Strongly Disagree					Strongly Agree	
1. Frequently initiates ideas	1	2	3	4	5	6	7
2. Is directed toward team goals	1	2	3	4	5	6	7
3. Manages conflict	1	2	3	4	5	6	7
4. Demonstrates support for others	1	2	3	4	5	6	7
5. Displays openness	1	2	3	4	5	6	7
6. Exhibits proper demeanor in decision making	1	2	3	4	5	6	7

Exercise 11

General Peer Feedback

Answer the following questions to provide feedback to the team member indicated. Check the number that you believe represents the usual behavior of that team member. The farther away from the middle (4), the stronger the team member's behavior.

Name: _____

IN MY OPINION THIS PERSON:	Strongly Disagree						Strongly Agree
1. Frequently initiates ideas	1	2	3	4	5	6	7
2. Is directed toward team goals	1	2	3	4	5	6	7
3. Manages conflict	1	2	3	4	5	6	7
4. Demonstrates support for others	1	2	3	4	5	6	7
5. Displays openness	1	2	3	4	5	6	7
6. Exhibits proper demeanor in decision making	1	2	3	4	5	6	7

Detach at perforation

Exercise 12

Detailed Peer Evaluation

Behavioral objectives:

To provide you with a personal, frank assessment of your performance as a team member.

Instructions:

Complete the peer evaluation form on the next page by assigning and justifying a grade for each team member. Guidelines for assigning grades are indicated below.

Do not evaluate yourself. Be specific and justify the grade assigned. Do not use generalities such as "we all contributed equally," "everyone worked hard," etc. Use the back of this page to specifically justify your evaluation of each individual. You evaluation is confidential.

Grade	Requirement
90–100	Attended all meetings. Was on time, well prepared, and actively contributed to the team.
80–90	Missed a maximum of one meeting or was late to a meeting. Was prepared and actively contributed most of the time.
70–80	Either missed more than one meeting or did not actively contribute to meeting (i.e., did not consistently move the conversation forward in a positive manner).
60–70	Had an attitude problem, or missed meetings, or was not prepared, or did not contribute to the conversation.
60 & lower	Explain reasons.

Exercise 12

Detailed Peer Evaluation

Member	Grade	Member	Grade

Who contributed the least? Why?

Who contributed the most? Why?

Comments on evaluations:

Detach at perforation

Exercise 13

Self-Assessment

It is always difficult to accept feedback regarding our behavior, particularly if the feedback is not what we expected. After reading the peer feedback evaluations, spend a moment in self-reflection.

Complete the following self-assessment checklist. Be "hard" on yourself. This is a private learning exercise, and no one else will see the results.

Self-Assessment of Your Team Skills						
IN A MEETING, I: Never						Often
1. Suggest new ideas or new courses of action	1 2 3 4 5 6 7					
2. Present the reasons behind my opinions	1 2 3 4 5 6 7					
3. Ask others for information and/or opinions	1 2 3 4 5 6 7					
4. Encourage other members to contribute	1 2 3 4 5 6 7					
5. Pull together and summarize ideas presented	1 2 3 4 5 6 7					
6. Try to find areas of agreement when conflicting points of view are expressed	1 2 3 4 5 6 7					
7. Dominate discussions	1 2 3 4 5 6 7					

Exercise 13

What is your best (most positive) behavior that helps the team?

What is the behavior that you should change (do less of) in your team?

Detach at perforation

Chapter 6

Understanding How We Think

Have you ever analyzed your beliefs? It is useful to do so, because your beliefs influence your actions, which influence your effectiveness in a team. Participation, empowerment, teamwork, and commitment hinge on one key factor: trust. An organization with a climate of little trust has to solve that problem before the issue of quality improvement can be addressed.

Developing Trust

Trust is based on honesty, but simply being honest and practicing the golden rule is not enough. A model of principle-centered leadership proposed by Covey includes the principles of trust, empowerment, and alignment. Covey believes that the key to effective teams is to align the corporate culture and values with these universal principles.

We can start the process of increasing trust by understanding how our thoughts, which are often expressed through our actions, impact others. Trust is won by knowing yourself, letting others see who you are, and by being willing to know who they are.[1] Trust is personal, and it depends on you, not the organization.

Do you work for the good of the organization? Most people would answer yes to this question. Do you then, however, do everything possible to protect your personal turf? Are issues based on merit, or is your perception colored by your ambitions? If so, you cannot possibly expect people to trust you.

Do you freely share information with members of the team, or do you deliberately (or subconsciously) withhold a few points so that you can "look good" to a superior? If people believe that you have their best interests in mind, they will excuse gaps in information, but the deliberate omission of critical information puts you back to square one in terms of trust.

Does management stress cost reduction, yet make expensive investments that in the eyes of the employees are questionable? If so, then employees really cannot be expected to try to save a few dollars when management appears to be extravagant. Managers should take employees into their confidence and make every effort to explain the central purpose of major expenditures and how these fit into the organizational vision. That is, employees must believe that decisions are not being made in a vacuum.

Do emergency conditions dictate a change in leadership style? If so, explain why. Employees need emotional stability in the workplace. If market conditions force a temporary autocratic style, a moment of explanation will enable the employees involved to understand why.

In fact, management must keep employees informed of all activities affecting the company, rather than just when they are forced to do so. Employees should be treated as intelligent colleagues, with honest, frank communication, so that their trust is earned.

Your fellow team members depend on you. When a major error occurs, it should of course be corrected. Remember, however, Dr. Deming's central point: Management owns the system and must assume responsibility for what occurs. Therefore, if management protects employees when things go wrong, respect will be earned and morale as well as the working environment will be improved.

Colored Hat Thinking

In order to improve our effectiveness as team members, we need to develop an understanding of how we and others think. The use of colors as an aid to thinking has been around for a long time, because colors are easy to associate with certain emotions.

Wearing colored hats[2] when role playing helps to overcome defense mechanisms. The colored hats permit us to envision and say things that we could not otherwise say without appearing foolish. That is, use of the colored hats allows the wearer to focus on one aspect of a thought process at a time. The wearer does not have to be concerned with objectivity when expressing his or her viewpoint. The wearer is simply portraying the thinking represented by the colored hat.

Hats also establish rules for the "game" of thinking. People are very good at learning the rules of the game, and it then becomes a powerful method for improving the thought process. Eventually, a person should be able to switch in and out of "hats" with ease during a discussion.

Hat Colors and Functions

White Hat **Mr. Clean**	White is neutral and objective. The white hat is concerned with objective facts and figures.
Red Hat **The Alarmist**	Red suggests alarm, anger (seeing red), rage, and emotion. The red hat gives the emotional view.
Purple Hat **The Pessimist**	Purple covers the gloomy and negative aspects. The purple hat reflects why something cannot be done.
Yellow Hat **Susie Sunshine**	Yellow is sunny, positive, and optimistic. It indicates new ideas, creativity, and moving forward.
Blue Hat **Cool Hand Luke**	Blue is cool. It suggests control and organization of the thinking process. The blue hat defines the problem and summarizes the contributions of others.

In practice, the hats are always referred to by their colors and never by their functions. There is a good reason for this. If you ask someone to give his or her emotional reaction to something, you are unlikely to get an honest answer because people think it is wrong to be emotional. The term "red hat" is neutral, however. You can ask someone to "take off the red hat" or "take off the purple hat for a moment" more easily than you can ask that person to stop being emotional or stop being negative.

Endnotes

1. For more information on trust, see the article by Perry Pascarella, "15 Ways to Win People's Trust," *Industrial Week,* pp. 47–53, Feb. 1, 1993.
2. The use of colors as an aid in understanding how we think is based on the German text by Dr. Max Luscher entitled *The Luscher Color Test* (translated and edited by Ivan Scott, New York: Simon and Schuster, 1969). Dr. Luscher's test uses colors to reveal personalities. Dr. Edward deBono expanded this early work into a concept called Six Hat Thinking, which he used in role playing.

Exercise 14

Norm Violation

Behavioral objectives:

To develop an understanding as to how we think, in particular what color thinking we normally assume.

Instructions:

Think about a group in which you have previously been a member. Identify a situation when either you or someone in the group did something that the group found unacceptable (i.e., violated a group norm). In the space provided, (1) indicate the norm that was violated, (2) the member's action that violated the action, and (3) how the group responded.

Take ten minutes to identify two such norms in the space provided on the next page. After you have completed your description, get together in your team. Each member is to read a norm, violation, and group response. Using the hat technique, identify which color hat the group was wearing in the "group response."

Detach at perforation

Exercise 14

Norm Violation		
Norm	**Violation**	**Group Response**

Detach at perforation

Exercise 15

Future Workplace

Instructions:

You have been sent to the future and the year is 2025. What will it be like to work for an organization? Take ten minutes to write out your description of the working conditions. Use the form provided on the next page.

After you have completed your descriptions, get together in your team. Use the hat technique to generate a consensus on at least four major ideas. If you do not have colored hats available, be prepared to identify what color you are assuming in the conversation.

Exercise 15

Future Workplace

Describe a typical day in the life of an office worker in a government agency.

Describe a typical day in the life of a manager in that same agency.

Detach at perforation

Exercise 16

University President

Instructions:

What would you do if you were president of the college or university you are attending? Why would you propose such action? Take ten minutes and write down four of your best ideas in the space provided on the next page.

After you have completed your description, get together in your team. Use the hat technique to generate a consensus on at least four major action items. Be prepared to defend your selections. If you do not have colored hats available, be prepared to identify what color you are assuming in the conversation.

Exercise 16

University President

What would you do if you were president of your university?

1.

2.

3.

4.

Detach at perforation

Chapter 7

Member Service Roles

In this chapter, team members will be asked to pay particular attention to three different roles: the team participant, leader, and observer. These roles should be rotated each time the team meets to ensure that all team members gain experience in all roles.

The role of a **team participant** is to actively discuss ideas and to help move the conversation forward. The key word here is **actively**. Do not sit idly and quietly on the sidelines. If you are going to be a team member, you must actively participate in the discussions.

The second role is that of the **leader**. The leader directs and leads the flow of the conversation. The leader does **not** engage in active discussion. The role of the leader, along with all other roles, is to be reassigned at the end of each meeting.

The third role is that of an **observer**. An observer watches or observes the teamwork process and discusses these observations at the end of each meeting. The observer does not participate in the discussion, but records what occurs using an Observer's Recording Form. These observations are objectively discussed (i.e., only reporting the facts) at the end of each meeting so that the team can improve its interactions.

The Observer's Recording Form is used to record participants' interactions when solving team exercises. After an exercise is completed, the observer presents his or her findings to the team, without emotion and without passing judgment. Team members discuss these findings in order to learn how to improve their effectiveness.

Exercise 17

Declining Enrollments

Behavioral objectives:

To assign specific team roles to team members and to keep track of their contributions through an observer. The observer's report is discussed at the end of the session so that team members learn how to improve their group processes.

Instructions:

A business school at a major university has just had a 12% decrease in enrollment. The school has always experienced increasing enrollments, and the decline is of major concern to the Dean. After interviewing several business leaders, the Dean is convinced that the decline represents a fundamental shift in student values and further decreases are likely.

Use the hat technique to come up with a specific written proposal to solve this problem. All team members (other than the observer) are to actively participate. The observer is to sit where he or she can see all group members and is to complete the group observation form.

© St. Lucie Press

Exercise 17

Declining Enrollments

Observer's Recording Form: Participant Interactions												
		Participant Names										
Hat Colors	White												
	Red												
	Purple												
	Yellow												
	Blue												

Date:

Comments:

Observer:

Team #:

Assignment:

Exercise 18

QI Project

Time limit:

20 minutes

Instructions:

A group of students have been asked to undertake a Quality Improvement (QI) project, which will be a significant portion of their grade. The problem is that the instructor has left it up to the team to decide what the project should be and to determine the scope of the project.

Appoint a new leader and a new observer. First, use the hat technique to come up with specific, written proposals for a team QI project. Then, rank the proposals (there can be more than one). All team members (other than the observer) are to actively participate in the team discussion. The observer is to sit where he or she can see all group members and is to complete the group observation form.

Exercise 18

QI Project

Observer's Recording Form: Participant Interactions											
		Participant Names									
Hat Colors	White										
	Red										
	Purple										
	Yellow										
	Blue										

Date:

Comments:

Observer:

Team #:

Assignment:

Detach at perforation

Exercise 19

Community Leader

Time limit: 15 minutes

Instructions:

You have five minutes to rank the top five characteristics that you feel are most important for a community leader (1 is most important, 5 is least important). After ranking the characteristics, get together in your team. Appoint a new leader and a new observer. Use the hat technique to reach a consensus ranking. The observer is to sit where he or she can see all group members and is to complete the group observation form.

Important Characteristics for a Community Leader		
Characteristic	**Your Answer**	**Team Consensus**
Interest in people		
Intelligence		
Grasp of local issues		
Good socializer		
Attractive		
Sense of humor		
Community loyalty		
Politically "connected"		
Financial independence		
Good physical health		

Exercise 19

Community Leader

Observer's Recording Form: Participant Interactions											
		Participant Names									
Hat Colors	White										
	Red										
	Purple										
	Yellow										
	Blue										

Date:

Comments:

Observer:

Team #:

Assignment:

Detach at perforation

Exercise 20

Teenage Night Owl

Time limit:

20 minutes

Instructions:

You are a parent of a high school teenager. His grades have been marginal, and lately he has begun associating with a few friends you find "undesirable." He consistently stays out late every night, and recently he has been coming home at about 3:00 a.m. on Friday and Saturday nights.

As his parent, you feel that he is a good kid, but you want to place limits on his behavior, particularly his late hours. You have already restricted his use of your car, but this had no effect on his behavior.

Get together in your team and use the hat technique to generate a list of suggestions. If you do not have colored hats available, identify what color you are assuming before you make a comment.

Exercise 20

Teenage Night Owl

Observer's Recording Form: Participant Interactions												
		Participant Names										
	White												
Hat Colors	Red												
	Purple												
	Yellow												
	Blue												

Date:

Comments:

Observer:

Team #:

Assignment:

Detach at perforation

Chapter 8

Expanded Team Member Roles

The purpose of assigning specific service roles to team members is to establish a climate in which teams can learn how to improve their group processes. When teams learn how to improve themselves, they both increase their opportunity for success and become highly motivated.[1] In order to improve, teams must keep accurate notes of when they meet, the length of the meeting, who was in attendance, and what was discussed.

The team is to elect a member to fill each of the service roles described in this chapter. In class, the role of the trainer will be assigned to the instructor, and the resource person may not be required. **Team members must rotate the service roles each time the team meets.** This is necessary for members to gain an understanding of the team process.

Team Member Service Roles

Participant	Actively discusses ideas and helps carry out what should be done
Leader	Guides the group as a coordinator–facilitator
Recorder	Records pertinent ideas expressed and summarizes results at the end of each meeting
Observer	Observes the teamwork process and discusses these observations at the end of each meeting
Resource Person	Used when needed on a planned discussion and addresses specific needs (not a speech)
Time-keeper	Watches the clock, schedules meetings, and reports on how the team productively utilizes its time
Trainer	Utilizes intervention to assist the team in learning how to learn

After team members gain experience in each of these roles (this will only take a couple of exercises), the following roles will be required: (1) leader, (2) recorder–observer–timekeeper, and (3) participant. A resource person can be appointed as needed; however, notes of all team meetings must be kept (by the recorder). At the end of each team meeting, an observer's report must be given. All members should take this opportunity to appraise how they worked together and to identify areas for improvement.

Team Member Service Role: Participant

The team cannot function without active participation by all members. As team participants share more in team responsibilities (before, during, and after planning discussions and activities), the team should have less to do.

Participant responsibilities include:

■ Being prepared

■ Actively sharing ideas, without dominating the discussion

■ Listening carefully

■ Sharing ideas, experiences, and expertise

■ Building on each other's contributions

■ Helping with group functions: serving as leader, recorder, etc.

■ Being flexible in terms of schedules, including meeting times

---

Team Member Service Role: Leader

The team leader is a volunteer who accepts primary responsibility for directing, leading, and coaching the team's process. The team leader is **not** the person who knows the most about the subject at hand (that is the role of the resource person). The leader must recognize the essential worth of each person in the team and then attempt to get all members to work together as a team.

The role of the leader is as a servant to the team. The leader must make every effort to lead members in learning how to learn. The team leader is responsible for service to the team before, during, and after team activities.

Leader responsibilities include:

■ Making pre-meeting preparations

■ Finalizing and distributing the agenda

■ Helping establish, and then abiding by, team ground rules

■ Keeping the facilitator (in this case, the instructor) informed of progress

■ Moving the group to a quality outcome by:

   ■ Shared planning

   ■ Shared appraisal

   ■ Free, voluntary expression

   ■ Acceptance of members as valuable individuals

Team Member Service Role: Recorder

The recorder prepares a written account of the content of the discussion, the subjects discussed, and what the group said. The role of the recorder is more than a secretarial function of recording points and topics discussed. The recorder notes significant comments made concerning a topic and reports what occurred at the end of a meeting. The recorder should feel free to raise such questions as, "Is this the point you are making?"

Recorder responsibilities include:

■ Reporting the essence of what was said about each topic (do not try to report every point)

■ Recording the point that was made, **not** who said something

■ Recording points on which opinions differ

■ Recording points of agreement and decisions made

Team Member Service Role: Observer

The observer concentrates on the group interaction process and how the team conducts its business. The observer does not interrupt the meeting unless requested by the team to review the situation. After the meeting, the observer objectively summarizes what occurred in order to assist the team in identifying learning obstacles.

Observer responsibilities include:

■ Providing a report on the group processes that occurred

■ Being objective and limiting the report to what occurred, without inferring what should have been done

■ Sitting so that he or she is facing the group and can see all members

■ Making reference to the content of the discussions, but **not** keeping a record of what was said

---

If the participants disagree with the observer's comments, there is no need to become defensive. No two people see situations in the same way. The observer should be as objective as possible.

When you observe, consider the following teamwork process factors:

■ Spontaneity of participation

■ Balanced participation

■ Emotional atmosphere

■ Dependence on the discussion leader

■ Helping others communicate

■ Clarity of tasks and goals

■ Building upon each other's contributions

■ Quality of listening

■ Factors that blocked progress toward the goal

Team Member Service Role: Resource Person

A resource person can be used when required by a team, provided the team plans ahead. The person serving as a resource should be told in writing specifically what is needed, and he or she should be instructed to answer the issues of concern the group without giving a speech.

Team Member Service Role: Timekeeper

After conferring with the team leader, the timekeeper sets a time limit for the meeting and reminds members of the time remaining during the meeting. The timekeeper should attend meetings with a calendar in order to facilitate scheduling the next meeting. (The timekeeper's role is often combined with that of the recorder.)

In addition to watching the clock, the timekeeper reports how team members productively worked within the planned time and when time pressures forced the team into non-productive behavior. When reporting time usage, only facts should be reported. No value judgments as to the team's productive use of its limited time are to be made. **Note:** Time will always be limited; this is a fact of life that teams must deal with.

Timekeeper responsibilities include:

■ Watching the clock

■ Setting a time limit for the meeting

■ Reminding others of time remaining

■ Reporting time usage

■ Attending meeting with a calendar to facilitate scheduling the next meeting

---

Group Task Functions

In order for teams to improve their effectiveness, team members must be aware of when they perform various task functions. The contributions team members make to these functions should be discussed at the end of each team meeting.

Task Functions	Task Description
Initiating	Proposing tasks, defining problems, coordinating, clarifying, or suggesting an idea
Giving information	Providing facts or information to assist the team in making a decision
Energizing	Motivating the team to make a greater effort
Evaluating or criticizing	Judging the evidence and conclusions the team suggests

The assigned observer should objectively record the interactions that occurred during the meeting for each of the task functions shown. The participants' names are abbreviated (initials or first name) and written in the boxes at the top of the Task Observation Form.

The observer completes the Task Observation Form and summarizes the interactions at the end of the team meeting. The observer does **not** state what should have been done. It is up to the team to consider the interactions and figure out how to improve their process. **Note:** The recorder is responsible for keeping an account of the actual content of the discussion.

A Task Observation Form is shown on the next page. The observer should sit where he or she can see each person on the team.

Task Observation Form

	Participant Names									

Tasks											
	Initiating										
	Giving Information										
	Energizing										
	Evaluating/ Criticizing										

Date: **Observer:**

Endnote

1. Of all the books and articles written on the subject of individual and group motivation, perhaps those by Frederick Herzberg and Abraham Maslow are among the best. Maslow's article, "A Theory of Human Motivation (*Psychological Review,* Vol. 50, pp. 370–396, 1943), was an early attempt to understand motivation. Then, Herzberg's article, "One More Time: How Do You Motivate Employees?" (*Harvard Business Review,* pp. 56–57, Jan–Feb. 1968), initiated the so-called "job enrichment" movement of the 1970s. This enrichment movement was the precursor to the TQM movement in the 1980s.

Exercise 21

Improving Schools

Behavioral objectives:

To offer a process by which teams can learn how to learn. The team leader should call for the observer's report at the end of each session. It is the job of all team members to objectively analyze the facts reported by the observer and identify how they can improve their team performance.

Instructions:

Get together in your assigned team. Read the rules on improving performance in Chapter 9. Then, use brainstorming to generate ideas that can be used to improve the public high schools in your town. You have the following time limits:

Allocate your time as follows:	
Topic	**Time**
Organize yourself; assign members to roles	5 minutes
Brainstorm about a topic	10 minutes

After electing/assigning members to the service roles, write the name(s) of the team member(s) assigned each role in the space provided on the next page. Remember, these roles are to be rotated each time the team meets. The instructor will serve as the trainer, and a resource person will not be required. The instructor is there to assist the group in the process of learning how to learn and will **not** answer questions or provide additional information.

Detach at perforation

Exercise 21

Improving Schools

Service Role by Team Member	
Service Role	**Member Name(s)**
Participants	
Leader	
Recorder	
Timekeeper	
Observer*	

* Use the task-function observation form previously provided when performing this brain-storming exercise.

Ideas for tackling this problem:

Exercise 22

Improving Services

Time limit:

25 minutes

<table>
<tr><td colspan="2">Allocate your time as follows:</td></tr>
<tr><td align="center">Topic</td><td align="center">Time</td></tr>
<tr><td>Organize yourself; assign members to roles</td><td>5 minutes</td></tr>
<tr><td>Select an industry or organization</td><td>10 minutes</td></tr>
<tr><td>Brainstorm about how to improve services</td><td>10 minutes</td></tr>
</table>

Instructions:

Get together in your assigned team. Elect/assign members to the service roles and record their names on the form provided. Be sure to rotate assignment of roles.

Your assignment is to select a service organization (other than education) and brainstorm about ways to improve the services offered by the organization.

Exercise 22

Improving Services

Service Role by Team Member

Service Role	Member Name(s)
Participants	
Leader	
Recorder	
Timekeeper	
Observer*	

* Use the task-function observation form provided at the end of this chapter.

Service organization selected:

Suggestions for improving services:

Detach at perforation

Exercise 23

Good Teacher

You have five minutes to rank the top five characteristics that you feel are the most important for a good university teacher from the list of characteristics shown below (1 is most important, 5 is least important). After ranking the characteristics, get together in your team. Appoint a new leader and appoint a new observer, who will complete a task observation form.

Characteristics of a Good University Teacher		
Characteristic	**Your Answer**	**Team Consensus**
Up-to-date on subject matter		
Intelligence		
Openly admits his or her errors		
Emphasizes learning		
Sets high standards of academic achievement		
Sense of humor		
Does not allow sloppy work to get by		
Gives easy-to-follow lectures		
Classes are well-disciplined and orderly		
Encourages open discussion on assigned topics		

Detach at perforation

Task Observation Form

	Participant Names									
Tasks Initiating										
Giving Information										
Energizing										
Evaluating/ Criticizing										

Date: **Observer:**

Detach at perforation

Task Observation Form

	Participant Names									

Tasks	Initiating										
	Giving Information										
	Energizing										
	Evaluating/ Criticizing										

Date: **Observer:**

Chapter 9

Expanding Team Skills

You have been introduced to a number of different service roles and have been recording group interactions in order to develop an understanding of how people interact in teams. Teams, particularly beginning teams, have a tendency to become totally involved with the particular exercise at hand and fail to spend enough time addressing the actual group processes.

Phases of a Meeting

There are four major phases in conducting a meeting. All team members must understand what is expected of them in each of the following phases: (1) before the meeting, (2) during the meeting, (3) after the meeting but before the team leaves, and (4) after the meeting and the team has left.

Before the Meeting

Leader	Participant
Establish meeting date and time	Confirm attendance
Secure a meeting room	Be flexible regarding when you can meet
Define objectives of meeting in an agenda	Define your role at the meeting
Notify participants	Do any required homework

During the Meeting

Leader	Participant
Start on time	Arrive on time
Follow the agenda	Actively contribute to the discussion
Elicit balanced participation	Limit side conversations and distractions
Help resolve conflicts	Be open-minded to ideas
Clarify action to be taken	Listen to and respect the opinions of others
Try to achieve consensus, and do not resort to voting	Participate in consensus with an open mind

---

After the Meeting, but Before the Team Leaves

Leader	Participant
Ensure time for observer's report	Reflect on your actions
Summarize results	Give up personal ownership to team ownership
Ensure that roles are rotated and that participants accept new roles	Ask yourself what you have learned regarding group interactions
Introduce new leader and new observer	

After the Meeting and the Team Has Left

Leader	Participant
Reflect on balanced contribution, and if you were able to stay out of discussions	Take any action agreed to
Restore room and return equipment	Follow up on action items
Ensure that the recorder distributes meeting notes	Think about what you should do differently during the next team meeting

Improving Performance

When working as a member of a team, it is important to remember that your effectiveness is measured in terms of how you contribute to the team, and not how "good" your comments are. The key to improving your team performance is to develop respect for each team member and to develop good communication skills.

Particular skill is needed when giving constructive feedback. The first rule to follow is to give such feedback only when it is obvious that the performance of the team will be affected without it.

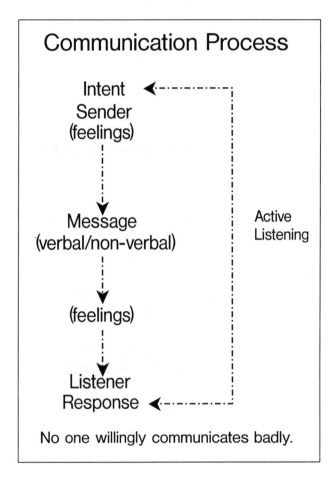

Communication Process

Intent
Sender
(feelings)

Message
(verbal/non-verbal)

(feelings)

Listener
Response

Active
Listening

No one willingly communicates badly.

Constructive Feedback Guidelines

■ Give positive and negative feedback

■ Understand the context

■ Know how to give feedback
   Be descriptive
   Don't exaggerate
   Speak for yourself

■ Know how to receive feedback
   Listen carefully
   Ask questions for clarity
   Acknowledge valid points
   Carefully consider the points
   Don't get angry

The most common mistake made in giving "constructive" feedback is giving only negative feedback. People like to feel good about themselves and what they do. If the only time someone hears from you is when something is going wrong, then your message will be delivered to a defensive person who will not be receptive.

More than one human relations author has summed up a good philosophy of communication: Catch someone doing something right and thank the person. Accentuate the positive; the positive is appreciated and is more likely to produce desirable results.

Common Group Problems

The following are examples of typical problems encountered by a team. A few suggestions are given for each group problem, but do not overlook the obvious: the power of the group itself. A group can begin functioning effectively as a team only when members can openly offer suggestions for means to improve their effectiveness. That is, each team member must be aware of these common group problem and must take an active role in resolving the issues.

Talkative Team Member

It is only natural for some people to want to be the center of attention and to feel that they have the best and most practical idea. However, the time a team can devote to discussion is limited. Each person on the team must be encouraged to participate equally, or members will not buy into the decisions reached. One person cannot be allowed to consistently dominate the discussion.

Suggestions:

■ Have the team leader point to a specific team member and ask, "We haven't heard from you. Do you have any ideas?"

■ The team leader could state, "I'd like to hear what others have to say."

■ The observer's report should clearly point out a lack of balanced participation. The reason for this lack of balance should be discussed.

Dominant Team Member

All team members must be treated with equal respect and courtesy. If one member exercises a dominant influence, perhaps due to higher rank in the organization, an assertive personality, or greater technical expertise, participation of other team members may be inhibited.

Suggestions:

■ The leader and other team members must reinforce that no ideas are "sacred" or "off limits."

■ Remind the team of the importance of consensus when making decisions. This cannot occur unless everyone's ideas are given a fair hearing.

■ Talk to the person before the next meeting and point out that although his or her expertise is needed, everyone's opinions must be honored.

Reluctant Participant

Some groups include members who rarely have anything to say and rarely make a contribution. If you talk privately to such a member, he or she is likely to say, "I will tell you if I have anything to contribute."

Suggestions:

■ Ask direct questions such as, "Mary, what do you suggest?"

■ When the observer's report is given, specifically address the non-contributor by name and ask, "What can we do to solicit your ideas."

■ If this behavior does not change and if the member provides a marginal contribution to the team in executing team decisions, then consideration should be given to removing the person from the team.

Argumentative Team Members

All too often, a couple of people in a group may personally dislike one another. That is understandable, and if they exercise professional courtesy in accomplishing their task, the differences in personalities can be ignored. However, if the individuals treat every discussion as an opportunity to prove their superiority rather than discuss the issues, the team will be ineffective. These clashes will not disappear. In fact such feuds will outlast the team.

The best way to handle this problem is to exercise caution when selecting team members and avoid placing known adversaries on the same team.

Suggestions:

■ Get the adversaries to discuss the issues away from the group.

■ Point out the disruptive effect of arguments.

■ Push the team members and the adversaries to establish ground rules for managing their discussion.

■ If nothing works, disband the team before too much time and effort are wasted.

Lack of Focus

A lack of focus, floundering, or not knowing what to do next can easily occur from time to time with any team.

Suggestions:

■ Review the mission (objectives) of the team.

■ Identify what is holding up the group: missing data, lack of expertise, lack of support, general feelings, etc.

■ Ask each person to suggest what he or she thinks is needed so the team can progress to the next stage.

■ Ask the group to critically analyze how the project is progressing.

In working together as team members, what can be done to overcome some of these blocks?

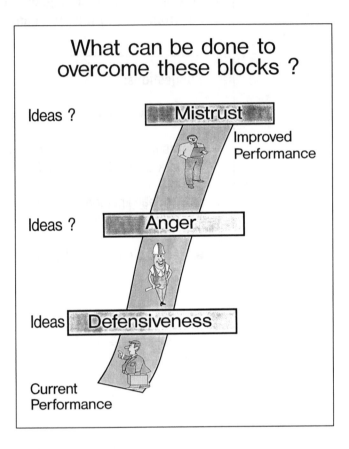

Remember, as previously stated, you will have to change **your** behavior to improve team effectiveness. Use this opportunity to improve your team effectiveness.

Exercise 24

General Wainwright

Behavioral objectives:

To practice learning how to improve our performance in teams. A team learns how to learn when members can openly discuss how to improve their performance as a team.

Instructions:

It is 1941, and General "Hawk" Wainwright, Commander of the U.S. Air Force, needs fighter planes. Your team is to produce aircraft according to his top-secret plans (see below).

You will be paid for each flight-certified aircraft, but fined for each crash and for each work-in-process plane at the end of the time period.

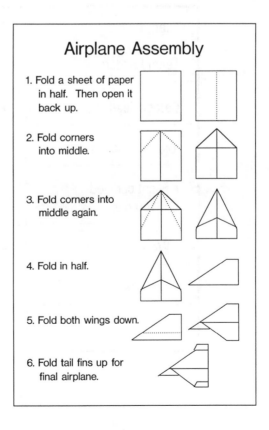

Airplane Assembly

1. Fold a sheet of paper in half. Then open it back up.

2. Fold corners into middle.

3. Fold corners into middle again.

4. Fold in half.

5. Fold both wings down.

6. Fold tail fins up for final airplane.

Exercise 24

Production bids are in units of 5 (such as 5, 10, 15, etc.) planes that pass flight certification. A crash is defined as a plane that does not "hit" the wall area designated by the instructor. All crashed planes are unrecoverable.

The observer (who must complete the task-function observation form provided at the end of this chapter) may **not** engage in production. Your team has five minutes to decide on and submit your aircraft production worksheet (for the current production round) or the team is ruled unsuitable for government production. When the General says, "Up we go into the wild blue yonder," you have 15 minutes to complete production, including flight certification.

Aircraft Production Worksheet			
Team #:	Team Observer:		
Team Leader:	Team Timekeeper:		
Categories/Figures	Round #1	Round #2	Round #3
"Bid" production units			
+ Flight certified @ $100 each			
– Work in Process	–$50 each	–$100 each	–$100 each
– Crashes	–$50 each	–$100 each	–$200 each
Profit			

Detach at perforation

© St. Lucie Press

Exercise 25

Team Assessment

Get together in your assigned team. Elect a team member to gather the answers to the following questions, summarize the responses, and report back to the team at the next meeting. This person should be someone who has not recently served in a team function and who did not previously summarize this team assessment survey.

Answer the questions on the next page to find out if your team meetings are improving. Please choose the one number that best matches how you feel about the statement. The farther away from the middle (4), the stronger your feeling about the statement.

Exercise 25

Team Assessment

IN MY OPINION:	Strongly Disagree					Strongly Agree	
1. This was an effective meeting	1	2	3	4	5	6	7
2. I clearly understood the team goals for this meeting	1	2	3	4	5	6	7
3. The team stayed on track in working toward its goals	1	2	3	4	5	6	7
4. The team considered my contributions	1	2	3	4	5	6	7
5. I felt free to express my opinions and make a contribution to the group	1	2	3	4	5	6	7
6. Conversation was balanced among members	1	2	3	4	5	6	7
7. I was satisfied with this meeting	1	2	3	4	5	6	7

Detach at perforation

Exercise 26

Now What?

You have crashed in a private plane and the pilot never filed a flight plan. No one even knows you are gone. There is absolutely no hope of anyone attempting to look for you. You are the only survivor, and you are totally lost, alone in the desert, miles from anywhere. The days are hot, and the nights are cold. You have decided to walk out, facing the sun, to look for help. You know the journey will be very long and difficult. You only have the minimum equipment specified.

Your task is to take ten minutes to consider the questions asked on the next page and record your answers in the space provided. Then get together in your assigned team, discuss the options, reach a consensus, and record the team consensus in the space provided. Do not change your answer on the recording sheet.

Exercise 26

Now What?

Condition	Your Answer	Team Consensus
You have the items listed below, which were not destroyed in the plane crash. Rank the items in order of importance for the journey you are going to take. a. A large, professional lumberjack's ax b. A small bottle of salt tablets c. A small cosmetic mirror d. A man's hat		
The second day of your journey, you come across an abandoned prospector's hut. The following items were found in the hut. Rank the items in order of importance for your continued journey. a. One gallon of 190-proof gin b. One baseball bat c. A box of kitchen matches		
The day is very hot and dry. There is a quart of water in your canteen, and you should: a. Ration it to a cup a day b. Wait until night, and then drink what you think you need c. Drink as much as you think you need when needed		
It is 4:00 p.m. and this is the third day you have been in the desert. You have clearly seen a city in the distance for the past half hour, including buildings and cars. All of a sudden, there is a puff of smoke, and a real, live genie appears. The genie tells you that you can select one of the following options as a wish. Which option should you select? a. He will place $5 million dollars in gold in your outstretched arms b. He will transport you to the nearest city c. He will go away if you tell him you don't believe in genies		

The third question in this exercise was adapted from the "Wilderness Survival Work Sheet" in *The 1976 Annual Handbook for Group Facilitators,* edited by J. William Pfeiffer and John E. Jones (La Jolla, Calif.: University Associates), 1976.

Detach at perforation

Task Observation Form											
		Participant Names									
Tasks	**Initiating**										
	Giving Information										
	Energizing										
	Evaluating/ Criticizing										

Date: **Observer:**

Task Observation Form

		Participant Names										
Tasks	**Initiating**											
	Giving Information											
	Energizing											
	Evaluating/ Criticizing											

Date: **Observer:**

Detach at perforation

Chapter 10

Teams, Teams, and More Teams

There are five major types of Quality Improvement (QI) teams: quality circles, task teams, cross-functional project teams, functional teams, and self-directed (or self-managed) teams. A sixth type—designed teams—will be added to this list. Entire books have been devoted to discussing teams and how their effectiveness can be improved.[1] It is not the purpose of this chapter to duplicate this wealth of knowledge, but rather the purpose is to highlight a few major factors that can be used to improve team effectiveness.

The Reason for Specialized Teams

The purpose of any team is to bring the thinking of a group of people to concentrate on solving a common problem. Teams can also provide a method by which consumer and employee viewpoints can be identified and discussed. Specialized teams have been developed to meet specific organizational needs. In the following sections, particular attention will be paid to identifying the conditions under which each type of team is effective.

Special-purpose teams do not occur by chance. They must be planned in advance to meet specific organizational needs. A good beginning point is for management and team members to understand the different types of teams that are available.

When used correctly, teams improve productivity through greater motivation and improved communication. Teams also reduce the overlap common in organizational structures. This is in part due to the integrative systems approach followed by many teams in the attainment of a common purpose.[2]

Quality Circles

The most common form of an organizational method for employee involvement, other than suggestion programs, is quality circles. A quality circle is defined as a small group of employees doing similar or related work, who meet regularly to identify, analyze, and solve problems relating to product and process quality. Their interest often extends to general operations improvements, in both manufacturing and services.[3]

By definition, quality circles are limited to small groups, and they are not involved in cross-functional issues. The concept reached its peak in the United States during the early 1980s but never achieved the potential benefits that the Japanese quality circles realized. Quality circles in the United States were not integrated with the goal setting and strategic planning processes. They also were not well integrated with the management systems in many organizations, which led to their early demise.

Task Teams

A task team is the simplest form of team structure and is a modification of the quality circle concept. Membership on the team is either elected or appointed, and the team is then assigned a well-defined task. Task teams are temporary in nature and work related, and membership is normally comprised of people from the same department. Task teams can exist at any level and, in many cases, are assigned the topic to be resolved. Quality circles, on the other hand, are free to choose their own subject, but this choice is, of course, restricted to their own functional area.

Advantages:

It is quick and easy to form a task team. Because everyone reports to the same administrative structure, minimal coordination is required.

Disadvantages:

Most meaningful changes or ideas cut across functional lines. Because membership is from within one function (department), approval must be obtained by going up the hierarchy. This limits the team's effectiveness in developing and/or implementing meaningful changes.

Cross-Functional Project Teams

Cross-functional project teams are comprised of members from different departments who are assigned an important but relatively well-defined task. Issues are discussed in project teams, but the team members typically must obtain department approval on issues before committing departmental resources. This team approach provides the lateral coordination usually missing in most hierarchical organizational forms and is a useful strategy for linking different and diverse activities. Cross-functional project teams are also useful in breaking down the barriers between functional entities, provided, of course, that the functional department management is receptive to changes.

Advantages:

Existing management feels more comfortable with project teams than with functional teams because the exact nature of the project is known and approval cycles are well defined.

Disadvantages:

Because project team members are "bound" to their departments, there is little the team can do without obtaining approval. This tends to restrict the creativity of the team unless the ground rules are well defined in advance and the team has a strong sponsor on the executive committee.

Functional Teams

Functional teams are assigned tasks that cut across functional lines (i.e., cut across departmental or other authoritative lines). Functional teams are comprised of representatives from different departments, and the team is given a charge by top management to develop proposals and revise work systems without obtaining departmental approval. They are more permanent than task teams and are given higher level and more important assignments. Functional teams need to be coordinated by a facilitator who reports to a quality council. The facilitator, working with multiple functional groups, helps to ensure that the group is progressing toward completion of its assignment and that the group is exercising power consistent with its assignment.

Functional teams are frequently given assignments that require the power and authority of different functional units to be changed so that customer needs can be better meet. (See the case study on page 176 in the discussion of Quality Councils, in which a QI team proposed that marketing should deal directly with the production work force on prototype parts and eliminate other departments from the approval cycle to speed up delivery.) Care must be taken to ensure that functional teams concentrate on doing the job better and that they do not become bogged down in the political considerations that are inevitable in any organization.

Advantages:

Functional teams are useful in reducing the time to introduce new products by bringing together otherwise diverse groups such as Manufacturing, Marketing, and Engineering.

Disadvantages:

Functional teams are given decision-making authority, but frequently feel they still have to obtain approval from their home department, which may be counterproductive.

Self-Directed (Self-Managed) Teams

Self-directed teams (also called self-managed or empowered teams) are responsible for completing broad, work-related activities. These teams usually have control over their jobs in order to optimize the effectiveness of the entire process, instead of just individual activities. The teams are given an assignment of a broad scope of work to be accomplished, and then the team members themselves identify the specific steps to be completed. Self-directed teams are capable of organizing themselves, requesting support from the necessary functional units, and accomplishing the task without seeking departmental or higher administrative approval.

Self-directed team members typically perform all the tasks necessary to complete an entire job, including setting up work schedules and job assignments and providing feedback via peer evaluations. Dr. Juran believes that this type of team is the wave of the future and is one of the keys to economic competitiveness.

Self-directed teams are not required to conform to departmental approval or regulations. For example, a self-directed work team might be formed by an automobile manufacturer to develop a new sports car. The team would be comprised of representatives from the major departments. If the team members find that they can react quickly by working cross-functionally, then they are expected to do so without seeking approval.

Advantages:

Self-directed teams can adapt to and meet the needs of a rapidly changing environment.

Disadvantages:

Existing management often feels threatened by these teams because they have the authority to take action without obtaining approval. Team members often feel there is a lack of mutual trust with other employees and among themselves. This may prevent self-directed teams from operating at maximum effectiveness.

Design Teams

A special-purpose team called a design team is often used to provide leadership in developing ideas for organizational improvement. This team is similar to a self-directed team, but it concentrates on developing ideas rather than implementing production assignments.

A design team of six to ten employees is appointed by the quality council. The team often evaluates what other organizations are doing and then engages internal groups in discussions of ways to respond to customer demands.

Steps in Developing Design Teams

■ Organization is committed to finding a better way

■ Quality council/teams investigate what others are doing

■ Executive group clarifies the mission

■ Quality council appoints a design team

■ Read about similar groups and visit sites

■ Analyze environment, technology, and jobs

■ Discuss draft plan with involved groups

■ Make recommendations to quality council

■ Implement design and evaluate

The design team should concentrate on the elements of good service quality and redesign the organization to accomplish that objective.

Quality Council

A quality council (often called a steering committee) is needed to focus an organization's QI efforts. The council is composed of senior management, who oversee the various cross-functional task teams and assist in keeping the organization focused on continuous quality improvement. This council provides the structure needed to choose projects, assign and assist QI teams, and follow up on implementation. Without a formalized structure such as a council, quality ideas are typically discussed and then put on the back burner because most good ideas cut across functional lines.

A typical quality council is shown below. A senior member of the executive committee (such as the executive vice president) should chair the council, which is normally composed of department management. Because the executive vice president has numerous other duties, a facilitator is often assigned to coordinate with the various quality teams.

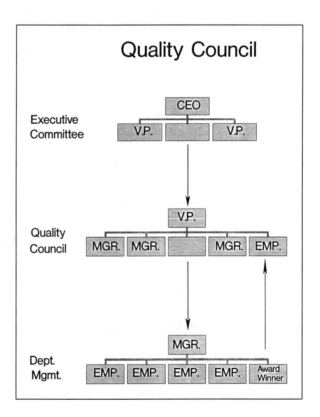

Facilitators meet with teams on a regular basis to ensure they stay on track and do not become bogged down. This is a time-consuming process, and hence the role of the facilitator quickly grows into a full-time job. Ideally, the facilitator should possess both technical QI skills and human relations/team-building skills so that assistance can be given to teams when needed.

The problem most organizations face is not in getting employees to offer improvement ideas, but rather in providing assistance in implementing ideas. After the council becomes established, employee membership can help others to understand the role of the council. One way of doing this is to create a two-month rotating position held by an employee who has received recognition for outstanding contributions to the organization's QI effort.

Successful Quality Councils

It is not unusual to find organizations that have a quality council, but it is unusual is to find a council that is successful in implementing and directing its QI programs. There are many reasons for this lack of success, the primary one being that quality councils are often composed of a group of executives who are used to operating autonomously.

A successful quality council must be an executive team dedicated to improving quality. The council is not a get-together of strong-willed people to "hammer out" agreements. The council must have a clearly defined function and the personal commitment of the CEO. It should be chaired by senior management and be comprised of management from the major departments in an organization.

An effective quality council is one whose members have helped in establishing the organization's mission and vision statement and who have a shared vision of the organization's future. Council members **must** be willing to change. They cannot take the attitude of defending their home turf or of representing their particular vested interests. Employees will quickly recognize political alliances, and if a certain group, say the engineering division, repeatedly exercises inflexibility, enthusiasm will be lost.

The following roles are typical of most successful councils:[4]

■ Create a sense of urgency for change

■ Establish direction

■ Engage, encourage, and empower employees

■ Demonstrate personal commitment

■ Implement a measurement system

■ Sponsor teams and provide resources

■ Perform management reviews

■ Coach and communicate

■ Recognize and reward

Case Study

Consider the following case study. Ajax Manufacturing Company specializes in producing high-volume parts to meet customer specifications. Ajax is profitable and sales are satisfactory, but a QI team felt that there was a better way of doing business. Senior technical marketing representatives (who are technically competent in the Ajax product line) call on key accounts on a routine basis. When these accounts are engaged in prototyping (creating a new product), Ajax salespeople interact closely with the buyers and design people in those firms.

A QI team recommended that minor customer changes could be recorded in pencil by the Ajax technical representatives on engineering documentation which they carry. The team recognized that the changes would have to be limited in scope and would not be a substitute for permanent engineering. The QI team found qualified and willing hourly employees in manufacturing who could produce to this documentation (which was faxed to them), without sacrificing quality. The revised parts would then be sent to the customer the next day by air mail. That is, changes would not first be sent to the engineering division to upgrade (revise) their engineering drawings. Nor would the revised drawings be sent to manufacturing engineering for tool and machine specification. Nor would production control schedule the changes. Nor would material control order the needed material (for one thing, there is no updated bill of material). Nor would quality control inspect the material or finished product. Nor would the part sent via inside transportation to shipping be routed in a standardized manner.

What would happen is that a skilled, senior-level machinist calls a local steel supply house for immediate delivery of the material needed, produces the prototype, and then calls a local overnight shipper to pick up the part as soon as it is available. The payoff for key customers during prototyping is a reduction in turnaround time from three weeks to three days.

How would a typical director of engineering react to the QI team's proposal, which virtually removes engineering from the design loop? Would he or she put obstacles in the path of such innovation? When it was actually time to implement the proposal, would the director of manufacturing and the director of quality really permit such empowerment? Would production control allow a machinist to "bump" schedules, even if for a few hours? Would purchasing permit an hourly employee to order material without first going through purchasing?

The effectiveness of a quality council is determined by how the council handles suggestions that cross functional lines. A moment's thought on this example can identify dozens of valid reasons why such a change cannot be accomplished, but only one reason why the proposal should be installed: the customer wants it.

Membership on a quality council must be seen as an opportunity for members to contribute. The importance of the tone established by the senior chair of the committee cannot be overemphasized. A council that works together as a team and adopts a positive, "we can make this new idea work" attitude sends a message to all members of the organization: your ideas really count.

Sustaining Continuous Quality Improvement

The questions confronting a quality council that is trying to sustain a continuous quality improvement movement are formidable. For example, how should rewards be given? One recommendation is to "shower" groups with dinner for two at a local restaurant. This is a gentle way for an organization to say "thank you," and it is further reinforced when the person dines with a "significant other."

Initially, indicators of quality should be considered in some manner, at least in annual performance reviews. These indicators may be relatively loose, consisting of factors such as the number of ideas submitted, working on QI teams, and the like. However, sooner or later, organizations should consider Juran's approach to sustaining a system for continuous quality improvement. Specific QI goals should be set, plans established to meet the goals, and progress measured. Progress toward meeting QI goals should be evaluated and incorporated into a formal annual performance review process.

Endnotes

1. An interesting book on the subject of organizational teams was written by John Ryan, entitled *The Quality Team Concept in Total Quality Control* (Milwaukee: ASQC Quality Press, 1992). The book looks at how various techniques, methods, and team-building tools fit together to restructure the organization's culture by taking a team approach to integrating TQM and JIT (Just-in-Time). Although written primarily for the manufacturing environment, its principles are equally effective in a service or government setting.

2. In their textbook *Principles of Total Quality,* Omachonu and Ross offer an interesting comparison between team membership and motivation. They point out that team membership, particularly in cross-functional teams, reduces organizational barriers and encourages an integrative systems approach to achieving common objectives. They offer several examples of success stories from teams in many different types of organizations.

3. See the work by Ross and Ross entitled *Japanese Quality Circles and Productivity* (Reston Publishing, 1982). These authors cover many aspects of the quality circle movement, including an action plan for starting the process. Also see Harrington and Rieker's article, "The End of Slavery: Quality Control Circles," *Journal for Quality and Participation,* pp. 16–20, March 1988.

4. For a complete description for the various quality council roles, see *Quality Council Handbook* by Frank Voehl (Strategy Associates, 1993). For a discussion on how to increase the effectiveness of a quality council, read "Planning for Successful Steering Committees" by Dan Ciampa (*Journal for Quality and Participation,* pp. 22–34, Dec. 1992).